Thomas Earl Petty, born in Gainesville, Florida, U.S., on October 20, 1950, was an American rock musician, singer, songwriter, multi-instrumentalist, and record producer. Petty performed as the lead singer of Tom Petty and the Heartbreakers. He was also a member and co-founder of the late 1980s supergroup the Traveling Wilburys, and his early band Mudcrutch.

Petty recorded a number of hit singles with the Heartbreakers and as a solo artist, sellling more than 80 million records worldwide, making him one of the best-selling music artists of all time. In 2002, Petty was inducted into the Rock and Roll Hall of Fame. He suffered cardiac arrest early in the morning of October 2, 2017 then died that night at the UCLA Medical Center in Santa Monica, California.

Petty was the first of two sons of Kitty (Avery) and Earl Petty, his interest in rock and roll music beginning at age ten, when he met Elvis Presley. In the summer of 1961, his uncle was working on the set of Presley's film Follow That Dream in nearby Ocala, inviting Petty to come down and watch the shoot. He instantly became an Elvis Presley fan, when returning home that Saturday, soon traded his Wham-O slingshot for a collection of Elvis 45s, with his friend Keith Harben.

In a 2006 interview, Petty said that he knew he wanted to be in a band the moment he saw the Beatles on The Ed Sullivan Show. "The minute I saw the Beatles on the Ed Sullivan Show—and it's true of thousands of guys—there was the way out. There was the way to do it. You get your friends and you're a self-contained unit and you make the music.

It looked like so much fun. It was something I identified with. I had never been hugely into sports. ... I had been a big fan of Elvis but I really saw in the Beatles that here's something I could do. I knew I could do it. It wasn't long before there were groups springing up in garages all over the place."

He dropped out of high school at age 17, to play bass with his newly formed band. In an interview with CBC in 2014, Petty stated that the Rolling Stones were "my punk music". Petty credited the group with inspiring him, by demonstrating that he and musicians like him could make it in rock and roll.

One of his first guitar teachers was Don Felder, a fellow Gainesville resident, who would later join the Eagles. As a young man, Petty worked briefly on the grounds crew for the University of Florida, but never attended as a student. An Ogeechee lime tree that he's said to have planted while employed at the university is now called the Tom Petty tree, although Petty has stated that he did not recall planting any trees. He also worked briefly as a gravedigger.

Petty overcame a difficult relationship with his father, who found it hard to accept that his son was "a mild-mannered kid, who was interested in the arts," subjecting him to verbal and physical abuse on a regular basis. Petty was extremely close to his mother, also remaining close to his brother, Bruce.

Petty started a band known as the Epics, later to evolve into Mudcrutch in 1967. Although the band, which featured future Heartbreakers Mike Campbell and Benmont Tench, were popular in Gainesville, their recordings went unnoticed by a mainstream audience. Their only single, "Depot Street", was released in 1975 by Shelter Records, but failed to chart.

After Mudcrutch split up, Petty reluctantly decided to pursue a solo career, with Tench forming his own group, whose sound Petty appreciated. Later Petty and Campbell collaborated with Tench and fellow members Ron Blair and Stan Lynch, in the first lineup of the Heartbreakers.

Their eponymous debut album gained very little popularity amongst American audiences, but had greater success in Britain. The single "Breakdown" was re-released in 1977, peaking at No. 40 in early 1978, after the band toured the UK, in support of Nils Lofgren. Their debut album was released by Shelter Records, distributed by ABC Records.

Their second album, You're Gonna Get It!, was the band's first to reach the Top 40, featuring the singles "I Need to Know" and "Listen to Her Heart". Their third album, Damn the Torpedoes, quickly went platinum, selling nearly two million copies, including their breakthrough singles "Don't Do Me Like That", "Here Comes My Girl" and "Refugee".

In September 1979, Tom Petty and the Heartbreakers performed at a Musicians United for Safe Energy concert, at Madison Square Garden in New York, their rendition of "Cry to Me" being featured on the resulting No Nukes album. In 1981 their Hard Promises album became a top-ten hit, going platinum, spawning the hit single "The Waiting," and featuring Petty's first duet, "Insider" with Stevie Nicks.

Bass player Ron Blair quit the group, being replaced by Howie Epstein on their fifth album, 1982's Long After Dark, their new line-up lasting until 1994. In 1985, the band took part in Live Aid, playing four songs at Philadelphia's John F. Kennedy Stadium. Southern Accents was also released that year.

The album included the hit single "Don't Come Around Here No More", which was produced by Dave Stewart. The song's video featured Petty dressed as the Mad Hatter, from the book Alice's Adventures in Wonderland, mocking and chasing Alice then cutting and eating her, as if she were a cake. The ensuing tour led to the live album Pack Up the Plantation: Live!

Following an invitation from Bob Dylan, Tom Petty and the Heartbreakers then joined him on his True Confessions Tour. They played some dates with the Grateful Dead in 1986 and 1987, the group also releasing Let Me Up (I've Had Enough), which included "Jammin' Me," which Petty wrote with Dylan.

In 1988, Petty joined George Harrison's group, the Traveling Wilburys, which also included Bob Dylan, Roy Orbison, and Jeff Lynne. The band's first song, "Handle with Care", was intended as a B-side of one of Harrison's singles, but was judged too good for that purpose, with the group deciding to record a full album, Traveling Wilburys Vol. 1.

A second Wilburys album, followed in 1990,, mischievously titled Traveling Wilburys Vol. 3, having been recorded without the recently deceased Orbison. The album was named Vol. 3 as a response to a series of bootlegged studio sessions, which had been sold as Travelling Wilburys Vol. 2. Petty incorporated Traveling Wilburys songs into his live shows, often playing "Handle with Care" in his concerts from 2003 to 2006, before adding "surprises" such as "End of the Line" to the set list of his 2008 tour.

In 1989, Petty released Full Moon Fever, which featured hits "I Won't Back Down", "Free Fallin'" and "Runnin' Down a Dream". It was nominally his first solo album, although several Heartbreakers and other well-known musicians participated: Mike Campbell co-produced the album with Petty and Jeff Lynne of Electric Light Orchestra, backing musicians including Campbell, Lynne, and fellow Wilburys Roy Orbison and George Harrison. Ringo Starr appeared on drums in the video for "I Won't Back Down", but they were actually played by Phil Jones.

Petty and the Heartbreakers reformed in 1991, releasing Into the Great Wide Open, which was co-produced by Lynne, including the hit singles "Learning To Fly" and "Into the Great Wide Open", the latter featuring Johnny Depp and Faye Dunaway in the music video.

Before leaving MCA Records, Petty and the Heartbreakers got together to record, live in the studio, two new songs for a Greatest Hits package: "Mary Jane's Last Dance" and Thunderclap Newman's "Something in the Air". This was Stan Lynch's last recorded performance with the Heartbreakers. Petty saying "He left right after the session, without really saying goodbye." The Greatest Hits went on to sell over ten million copies, receiving diamond certification by the RIAA.

In 1989, while still under contract to MCA, Petty secretly signed a lucrative deal with Warner Bros. Records, to which the Traveling Wilburys had already been signed. His first album on his new label, 1994's Wildflowers, Petty's second of three solo albums, included the singles "You Don't Know How It Feels", "You Wreck Me", "It's Good to Be King", and "A Higher Place". The album, produced by Rick Rubin, sold over three million copies in the US.

In 1996, Petty, with the Heartbreakers, released a soundtrack to the movie She's the One, starring Cameron Diaz and Jennifer Aniston. The album's singles were "Walls (Circus)" (featuring Lindsey Buckingham), "Climb that Hill", and a song written by Lucinda Williams, "Change the Locks". The album also included a cover of "Asshole", a song by Beck. The same year, the band accompanied Johnny Cash on Unchained, provisionally entitled "Petty Cash", for which Cash would win a Grammy for Best Country Album. Cash later covered Petty's "I Won't Back Down" on American III: Solitary Man.

In 1999, Tom Petty and the Heartbreakers released their last album with Rubin at the helm, Echo, reaching # 10 in the U.S. album charts. Two songs were released as singles in the U.S., "Room at the Top" and "Free Girl Now". Tom Petty and the Heartbreakers played "I Won't Back Down" at the America: A Tribute to Heroes, benefit concert for victims of the September 11, 2001 attacks. The following year, they played "Taxman", "I Need You" and "Handle with Care", having been joined for the last by Jeff Lynne, Dhani Harrison, and Jim Keltner, at the Concert for George, in honour of Petty's friend and former bandmate George Harrison.

Petty's 2002 release, The Last DJ, was an album-length critique of the practices within the music industry, peaking at # 9 on the Billboard 200 album chart in the US. The title track, inspired by Los Angeles radio personality Jim Ladd, bemoaned the end of the freedom that radio DJs once had, to personally select songs for their station's playlists. In 2005, Petty began hosting his own show "Buried Treasure," on XM Satellite Radio, on which he shared selections from his personal record collection.

In February 2006, Tom Petty and the Heartbreakers agreed to be the headline act at the fifth annual Bonnaroo Music and Arts Festival. Petty and the Heartbreakers' "30th Anniversary Tour" followed, featuring special guests including Stevie Nicks, Pearl Jam, the Allman Brothers Band, Trey Anastasio, the Derek Trucks Band, and the Black Crowes, who had also opened for Petty on their 2005 Summer Tour. Nicks would join Petty and the Heartbreakers on stage for "a selection of songs", including "Stop Draggin' My Heart Around".

In July 2006, Petty released a solo album titled Highway Companion, which included the hit "Saving Grace". It debuted at # 4 on the Billboard 200, which was Petty's highest chart position since the introduction of the Nielsen SoundScan system for tracking album sales in 1991. Highway Companion featured on the tour with the Heartbreakers in 2006, with performances of "Saving Grace", "Square One", "Down South" and "Flirting with Time". In 2006, A C hired Petty to perform in its National Basketball Association playoffs coverage.

During the summer of 2007, Petty reunited with his old bandmates Tom Leadon and Randall Marsh, along with Heartbreakers Benmont Tench and Mike Campbell, to reform his pre-Heartbreakers band Mudcrutch. The band had originally formed in 1967 in Gainesville, Florida, before relocating to California, where they'd released one single in 1974, before breaking up. The quintet recorded this self-titled new album of 14 songs that was released on April 29, 2008, an additional song "Special Place" being available on iTunes, if the album was pre-ordered. The band supported the album with a brief tour of California in the spring of 2008.

In 2007, artists as diverse as Willie Nelson, Lucinda Williams, Norah Jones, Lenny Kravitz, and Paul McCartney, paid tribute to Fats Domino on the double-CD covers set Goin' Home: A Tribute to Fats Domino. The album's sales helped buy instruments for students in New Orleans schools, also contributing to the building of a community centre in the city's Hurricane Katrina-damaged Ninth Ward. Petty and the Heartbreakers' contributed a critically acclaimed cover of Fats Domino's "I'm Walkin'" to the package.

On February 3, 2008, Tom Petty and the Heartbreakers performed during the halftime-show of Super Bowl XLII at the University of Phoenix Stadium. They played "American Girl", "I Won't Back Down", "Free Fallin'" and "Runnin' Down a Dream", in that order. "I Won't Back Down" was used in the closing credits of the coverage on BBC Two.

On May 30 2008, the band embarked on a North American Tour, with Steve Winwood performing as the opening act, joining Petty and the Heartbreakers on stage at some shows, starting on June 6, 2008, in Philadelphia, Pennsylvania. Winwood included his Spencer Davis Group hit "Gimme Some Lovin'", also occasionally performing his Blind Faith hit "Can't Find My Way Home".

The Live Anthology project by Tom Petty and the Heartbreakers, was announced nearly a year after Petty's record Extended Play Live with Mudcrutch. In November 2009, Petty told Rolling Stone that he was working on a new album with the Heartbreakers, saying, "It's blues-based. Some of the tunes are longer, more jam-y kind of music. A couple of tracks really sound like the Allman Brothers—not the songs but the atmosphere of the band."

The band's twelfth album, Mojo, was released on June 15, 2010, reaching # two on the Billboard 200 album chart. To promote the record, the band appeared as the musical guests on the finale of the 35th season of Saturday Night Live, on May 15, 2010. The release of Mojo was followed by a North American summer tour, which began on June 1, 2010.

In spring 2012, the band went on a world tour that included their first European dates in 20 years, with their first ever concerts in the Canadian provinces of Nova Scotia and Newfoundland and Labrador. Prior to the tour, five of the band's guitars, including two owned by Petty, were stolen from the band's practice space in Culver City, California in April, before being recovered by Los Angeles police the following week.

On July 29, 2014, Reprise Records released Tom Petty and the Heartbreakers' thirteenth studio album, Hypnotic Eye. The album debuted at # 1 on the Billboard 200, becoming the first Tom Petty and the Heartbreakers album to ever top the chart. On November 20, 2015, a channel called Tom Petty Radio debuted on SiriusXM.

Petty's first appearance in film took place in 1978, when he had a cameo in FM. He later had a small part in 1987's Made in Heaven, also appearing in several episodes of It's Garry Shandling's Show between 1987 and 1990, playing himself as one of Garry's neighbours. Petty was also featured in Shandling's other show, The Larry Sanders Show, as one of the Story within a story, final guests. In the episode, Petty got bumped from the show, nearly coming to blows with Greg Kinnear.

Petty appeared in the 1997 film The Postman, directed by and starring Kevin Costner, as the Bridge City Mayor, it being implied from the dialogue that he was playing a future history version of himself.

In 2002, he appeared on The Simpsons, in the episode "How I Spent My Strummer Vacation", along with Mick Jagger, Keith Richards, Lenny Kravitz, Elvis Costello, and Brian Setzer. In it, Petty spoofed himself, as a tutor to Homer Simpson on the art of lyric writing, composing a brief song about a drunk girl driving down the road, while concerned with the state of public schools. Later in the episode, he lost a toe during a riot.

Petty had a recurring role as the voice of Elroy "Lucky" Kleinschmidt, in the animated comedy series King of the Hill, from 2004 to 2009. In 2010, Petty made a five-second cameo appearance with comedian Andy Samberg, in a musical video titled "Great Day," featured on the bonus DVD, as part of The Lonely Island's new album Turtleneck & Chain.

Petty was a staunch guardian of his artistic control and artistic freedom, in 1979, having been involved in a legal dispute, when ABC Records was sold to MCA Records, refusing to be transferred to another record label without his consent. In May 1979, he filed for bankruptcy then was signed to the new MCA subsidiary, Backstreet Records.

In early 1981, the upcoming Tom Petty and the Heartbreakers album, which would become Hard Promises, was slated to be the next MCA release, with the new list price of $9.98, following Steely Dan's Gaucho and the Olivia Newton-John/Electric Light Orchestra Xanadu soundtrack.

This so-called "superstar pricing" was $1.00 more than the usual list price of $8.98. Petty voiced his objections to the price hike in the press, the issue becoming a popular cause among music fans. Non-delivery of the album and naming it Eight Ninety-Eight were considered, before MCA decided against the price increase.

In 1987, Petty sued tyre company B.F. Goodrich for $1 million, for using a song very similar to his song "Mary's New Car," in a TV advert. The agency that produced the commercial had previously sought permission to use Petty's song but was refused. A judge issued a temporary restraining order, prohibiting further use of the ad, the suit later being settled out of court.

It has been observed that the Red Hot Chili Peppers single "Dani California", released in May 2006, is very similar to Petty's "Mary Jane's Last Dance". Petty told Rolling Stone, "I seriously doubt that there is any negative intent there and a lot of rock 'n' roll songs sound alike. Ask Chuck Berry. The Strokes took 'American Girl' for their song 'Last Nite', and I saw an interview with them where they actually admitted it. That made me laugh out loud. I was like, 'OK, good for you' ... If someone took my song note for note and stole it maliciously, then maybe [I'd sue] but I don't believe in lawsuits much. I think there are enough frivolous lawsuits in this country, without people fighting over pop songs."

In January 2015, it was revealed that Petty and Jeff Lynne would receive royalties from Sam Smith's song "Stay with Me," after its writers acknowledged similarities between it and "I Won't Back Down". Petty and co-composer Lynne were awarded 12.5% of the royalties from "Stay with Me", and the names of Petty and Lynne, joined James John Napier, known professionally as Jimmy Napes, in the ASCAP song credit.

Petty clarified that he did not believe Smith plagiarized him, saying, "All my years of songwriting have shown me these things can happen. Most times you catch it before it gets out the studio door but in this case it got by. Sam's people were very understanding of our predicament and we easily came to an agreement".

Petty married Jane Benyo in 1974, having two daughters, Adria becoming a director, and AnnaKim Violette an artist, before they divorced in 1996. Benyo disclosed to Stevie Nicks that she had met Petty at "the age of seventeen." Nicks misheard Benyo, leading to Nicks' song "Edge of Seventeen". Petty married Dana York on June 3, 2001, having had a stepson, Dylan, from York's earlier marriage.

In May 1987, an arsonist set fire to Petty's house in Encino, California. Firefighters were able to salvage the basement recording studio and the original tapes stored there, as well as his Gibson Dove acoustic guitar but his signature grey top hat was destroyed. Petty later rebuilt the house with fire-resistant materials. Petty spoke in 2014 of the benefits from his practice of Transcendental Meditation.

Petty was found unconscious at his home, not breathing and in full cardiac arrest, early in the morning of Monday, October 2, 2017. He was taken to the UCLA Medical Center in Santa Monica, California, where he died at 8:40 pm PDT that evening. After reports of Petty's hospitalization, premature reports of his death spread widely, without official denial, until the band's management issued official confirmation shortly after Petty's actual death that Monday evening.

Petty owned and used a number of guitars over the years, from 1976 to 1982, his main instrument having been a sunburst 1964 Fender Stratocaster. He also used a number of Rickenbacker guitars from 1979 onward, notably a 1965 Rose Morris in 1993 and reissue of the Rose Morris in 1997, a 1967 360/12 and 1989 660/12TP. The Rickenbacker 660/12TP was designed by Petty, specifically the neck, featuring his signature from 1991 to 1997.

For acoustic guitars, Petty had a signature C.F. Martin HD-40, and wrote virtually all of his songs on a Gibson Dove acoustic, saved from his 1987 house fire. He also used a Gibson J-200 in a natural finish and a late 1970s Guild D25 12-string acoustic. Petty's later amplifier setup, featured two Fender Vibro-King 60-watt combos.

Awards and honours

In 1994, You Got Lucky, a Petty tribute album featuring such bands as Everclear and Silkworm was released. In April 1996, Petty received the UCLA's George Gershwin and Ira Gershwin Award for Lifetime Musical Achievement. The next month, Petty won the American Society of Composers, Authors and Publishers' Golden Note Award.

Tom Petty and the Heartbreakers received a star on the Hollywood Walk of Fame in 1999, for their contribution to the recording industry. In December 2001, Tom Petty and the Heartbreakers were inducted into the Rock and Roll Hall of Fame in New York.

Petty received the Billboard Century Award, the organization's highest honour for creative achievement, at a ceremony on December 6, 2005, during the Billboard Music Awards, at the MGM Grand Garden Arena in Las Vegas.

In September 2006, Tom Petty and the Heartbreakers received the keys to the city of Gainesville, Florida, where he and his bandmates either lived or grew up. From July 2006 until 2007, the Rock and Roll Hall of Fame in Cleveland, Ohio, featured an exhibit of Tom Petty items, much of the content having been donated by Petty, during a visit to his home by some of the Hall's curatorial staff.

Peter Bogdanovich's documentary film on Petty's career, titled Runnin' Down a Dream, premiered at the New York Film Festival in October 2007.

Discography

Solo

Full Moon Fever (1989)

Wildflowers (1994)

Highway Companion (2006)

with the Heartbreakers

Tom Petty and the Heartbreakers (1976)

You're Gonna Get It! (1978)

Damn the Torpedoes (1979)

Hard Promises (1981)

Long After Dark (1982)

Southern Accents (1985)

Let Me Up (I've Had Enough) (1987)

Into the Great Wide Open (1991)

Songs and Music from "She's the One" (1996)

Echo (1999)

The Last DJ (2002)

Mojo (2010)

Hypnotic Eye (2014)

with the Traveling Wilburys

Traveling Wilburys Vol. 1 (1988)

Traveling Wilburys Vol. 3 (1990)

with Mudcrutch

Mudcrutch (2008)

2 (2016)

Known professionally as **Bob Dylan**, born in Duluth, Minnesota, U.S. on May 24th, 1941, **Robert Allen Zimmerman** is an American singer, songwriter, musician, painter, and writer, having been influential in popular music and culture for more than five decades. Much of his most celebrated work dates from the 1960s, when he became a reluctant "voice of a generation," with songs such as "Blowin' in the Wind" and "The Times They Are a-Changin'", which became anthems for the civil rights and anti-war movements.

Leaving behind his initial base in the American folk music revival, his six-minute single "Like a Rolling Stone", recorded in 1965, widened the range of popular music. Dylan's lyrics have incorporated a wide range of political, social, philosophical, and literary influences, having defied existing pop music conventions and appealed to the burgeoning counterculture. Initially inspired by the performances of Little Richard and the songwriting of Woody Guthrie, Robert Johnson, and Hank Williams, Dylan has amplified and personalized musical genres.

His recording career, spanning more than 50 years, has explored the traditions in American song—from folk, blues, and country, to gospel, rock and roll and rockabilly, to English, Scottish, and Irish folk music, embracing even jazz and the Great American Songbook. Dylan has performed with guitar, keyboards, and harmonica.

Backed by a changing lineup of musicians, he has toured steadily since the late 1980s, on what has been dubbed the Never Ending Tour. His accomplishments as a recording artist and performer have been central to his career, but his songwriting is considered his greatest contribution. Since 1994, Dylan has also published seven books of drawings and paintings, and his work has been exhibited in major art galleries.

As a musician, Dylan has sold more than 100 million records, making him one of the best-selling artists of all time. He has also received numerous awards, including eleven Grammy Awards, a Golden Globe Award, and an Academy Award. Dylan has been inducted into the Rock and Roll Hall of Fame, Minnesota Music Hall of Fame, Nashville Songwriters Hall of Fame, and Songwriters Hall of Fame.

The Pulitzer Prize jury in 2008, awarded him a special citation for "his profound impact on popular music and American culture, marked by lyrical compositions of extraordinary poetic power." In May 2012, Dylan received the Presidential Medal of Freedom from President Barack Obama. In 2016, he was awarded the Nobel Prize in Literature "for having created new poetic expressions, within the great American song tradition".

Bob Dylan was born in St. Mary's Hospital on May 24, 1941, in Duluth, Minnesota, and raised in Hibbing, Minnesota, in the Mesabi Range, west of Lake Superior. He has a younger brother, David. Dylan's paternal grandparents, Zigman and Anna Zimmerman, emigrated from Odessa, in the Russian Empire (now Ukraine), to the United States, following the anti-Semitic pogroms of 1905.

His maternal grandparents, Ben and Florence Stone, were Lithuanian Jews, who arrived in the United States in 1902. In his autobiography, Chronicles: Volume One, Dylan wrote that his paternal grandmother's maiden name was Kirghiz, her family having originated from the Kağızman district of Kars Province, in northeastern Turkey.

Dylan's father, Abram Zimmerman – an electric-appliance shop owner – and mother, Beatrice "Beatty" Stone, were part of a small, close-knit Jewish community. They lived in Duluth until Robert was six, when his father caught polio, so the family returned to his mother's hometown, Hibbing, where they lived for the rest of Robert's childhood. In his early years he listened to the radio—first to blues and country stations, from Shreveport, Louisiana then later, when he was a teenager, to rock and roll.

Robert formed several bands while attending Hibbing High School. In the Golden Chords, he performed covers of songs by Little Richard and Elvis Presley. Their performance of Danny & the Juniors' "Rock and Roll Is Here to Stay" at their high school talent show, was so loud that the principal cut the microphone.

On January 31, 1959, three days before his death, Buddy Holly performed at the Duluth Armory. Seventeen year old Zimmerman was in the audience; in his Nobel Prize lecture, Dylan remembered: "He looked me right straight dead in the eye, and he transmitted something. Something I didn't know what and it gave me the chills."

In 1959, his high school yearbook carried the caption "Robert Zimmerman: to join 'Little Richard'." The same year, as Elston Gunnn, he performed two dates with Bobby Vee, playing piano and clapping. In September 1959, Zimmerman moved to Minneapolis, where he enrolled at the University of Minnesota, his focus on rock and roll giving way to American folk music. In 1985, he said:

"The thing about rock'n'roll, is that for me anyway, it wasn't enough... There were great catch-phrases and driving pulse rhythms... but the songs weren't serious or didn't reflect life in a realistic way. I knew that when I got into folk music, it was more of a serious type of thing. The songs are filled with more despair, more sadness, more triumph, more faith in the supernatural, much deeper feelings".

Living at the Jewish-centric fraternity Sigma Alpha Mu house, Zimmerman began to perform at the Ten O'Clock Scholar, a coffeehouse a few blocks from campus, becoming involved in the Dinkytown folk music circuit. During his Dinkytown days, Zimmerman began introducing himself as "Bob Dylan".

In his memoir, he said he hit upon using this less common variant for Dillon – a surname he had considered adopting – when he unexpectedly saw some poems by Dylan Thomas. Explaining his change of name in a 2004 interview, Dylan remarked, "You're born, you know, the wrong names, wrong parents. I mean, that happens. You call yourself what you want to call yourself. This is the land of the free."

In May 1960, Dylan dropped out of college at the end of his first year then In January 1961, he traveled to New York City, to perform there and visit his musical idol Woody Guthrie, who was seriously ill with Huntington's disease, in Greystone Park Psychiatric Hospital. Guthrie had been a revelation to Dylan, having influenced his early performances.

Describing Guthrie's impact, he wrote: "The songs themselves had the infinite sweep of humanity in them... [He] was the true voice of the American spirit. I said to myself I was going to be Guthrie's greatest disciple." As well as visiting Guthrie in hospital, Dylan befriended Guthrie's protégé Ramblin' Jack Elliott. Much of Guthrie's repertoire was channeled through Elliott, with Dylan paying tribute to him in Chronicles: Volume One.

From February 1961, Dylan played at clubs around Greenwich Village, befriending and picking up material from folk singers there, including Dave Van Ronk, Fred Neil, Odetta, the New Lost City Ramblers and Irish musicians the Clancy Brothers and Tommy Makem. New York Times critic Robert Shelton first noticed Dylan in a review of Izzy Young's production for WRVR, of a live twelve-hour Hootenanny on July 29, 1961, Dylan's first live radio performance:

"Among the newer promising talents deserving mention, are a 20-year-old latter-day Guthrie disciple, named Bob Dylan, with a curiously arresting, mumbling, country-steeped manner". In September, Shelton boosted Dylan's career further, with a very enthusiastic review of his performance at Gerde's Folk City. The same month Dylan played harmonica on folk singer Carolyn Hester's third album, which brought his talents to the attention of the album's producer, John Hammond, who signed Dylan to Columbia Records.

The performances on his first Columbia album, Bob Dylan, released March 19, 1962, consisted of familiar folk, blues and gospel songs, with two original compositions. The album sold only 5,000 in its first year, just enough to break even. Within Columbia Records, some referred to the singer as "Hammond's Folly" suggesting dropping his contract, but Hammond defended Dylan, having been supported by Johnny Cash.

In March 1962, Dylan contributed harmonica and back-up vocals to the album Three Kings and the Queen, accompanying Victoria Spivey and Big Joe Williams, on a recording for Spivey Records. While working for Columbia, Dylan recorded under the pseudonym Blind Boy Grunt, for Broadside, a folk magazine and record label. Dylan also used the pseudonym Bob Landy, to record as a piano player on The Blues Project, a 1964 anthology album by Elektra Records then as Tedham Porterhouse, Dylan played harmonica on Ramblin' Jack Elliott's 1964 album, Jack Elliott.

Dylan made two important career moves in August 1962, legally changing his name to Robert Dylan then signing a management contract with Albert Grossman. In June 1961, Dylan had signed an agreement with Roy Silver but in 1962, Grossman paid Silver $10,000, to become sole manager.

Grossman remained Dylan's manager until 1970, with a sometimes confrontational personality but being protective loyal. Dylan said, "He was kind of like a Colonel Tom Parker figure ... you could smell him coming." Tensions between Grossman and John Hammond led to Hammond's being replaced as producer of Dylan's second album, by the young African-American jazz producer, Tom Wilson.

Dylan made his first trip to the United Kingdom from December 1962 to January 1963. He'd been invited by TV director Philip Saville, to appear in a drama, Madhouse on Castle Street, which Saville was directing for BBC Television. At the end of the play, Dylan performed "Blowin' in the Wind", one of its first public performances but the film recording of Madhouse on Castle Street was destroyed by the BBC in 1968. While in London, Dylan performed at London folk clubs, including the Troubadour, Les Cousins, and Bunjies, also learning material from UK performers, including Martin Carthy.

By the time of Dylan's second album, The Freewheelin' Bob Dylan, in May 1963, he had begun to make his name as a singer and a songwriter. Many songs on this album were labeled protest songs, inspired partly by Guthrie and influenced by Pete Seeger's passion for topical songs, "Oxford Town", being an account of James Meredith's ordeal, as the first black student to risk enrollment at the University of Mississippi.

The first song on the Freewheelin' album, "Blowin' in the Wind", partly derived its melody from the traditional slave song, "No More Auction Block", while its lyrics questioned the social and political status quo. The song was widely recorded by other artists, becoming a hit for Peter, Paul and Mary.

Another Freewheelin' song, "A Hard Rain's a-Gonna Fall," was based on the folk ballad "Lord Randall". With veiled references to an impending apocalypse, the song gained more resonance when the Cuban Missile Crisis developed, a few weeks after Dylan began performing it. Like "Blowin' in the Wind", "A Hard Rain's a-Gonna Fall," marked a new direction in songwriting, blending a stream-of-consciousness, imagist lyrical attack, with traditional folk form.

Dylan's topical songs enhanced his early reputation, as he came to be seen as more than just a songwriter. Janet Maslin wrote of Freewheelin': "These were the songs that established [Dylan] as the voice of his generation—someone who implicitly understood how concerned young Americans felt about nuclear disarmament and the growing Civil Rights Movement: his mixture of moral authority and nonconformity, was perhaps the most timely of his attributes."

Freewheelin' also included love songs and surreal talking blues. Humour was an important part of Dylan's persona, the range of material on the album impressing listeners, including the Beatles. George Harrison said of the album, "We just played it, just wore it out. The content of the song lyrics and just the attitude—it was incredibly original and wonderful."

The rough edge of Dylan's singing was unsettling to some but an attraction to others. Joyce Carol Oates wrote: "When we first heard this raw, very young, and seemingly untrained voice, frankly nasal, as if sandpaper could sing, the effect was dramatic and electrifying." Many early songs reached the public through more palatable versions by other performers, such as Joan Baez, who became Dylan's advocate as well as his lover. Baez was influential in bringing Dylan to prominence, by recording several of his early songs then inviting him on stage during her concerts. "It didn't take long before people got it, that he was pretty damned special," said Baez.

Others who had hits with Dylan's songs in the early 1960s, included the Byrds, Sonny & Cher, the Hollies, Peter, Paul and Mary, the Association, Manfred Mann and the Turtles. Most attempted a pop feel and rhythm, while Dylan and Baez performed them mostly as sparse folk songs. The covers became so ubiquitous that CBS promoted him with the slogan "Nobody Sings Dylan Like Dylan."

"Mixed-Up Confusion", recorded during the Freewheelin' sessions with a backing band, was released as a single but then quickly withdrawn. In contrast to the mostly solo acoustic performances on the album, the single showed a willingness to experiment with a rockabilly sound. Cameron Crowe described it as "a fascinating look at a folk artist, with his mind wandering towards Elvis Presley and Sun Records."

In May 1963, Dylan's political profile rose, when he walked out of The Ed Sullivan Show. During rehearsals, Dylan had been told by CBS television's head of program practices that "Talkin' John Birch Paranoid Blues," was potentially libelous to the John Birch Society, so rather than comply with censorship, Dylan refused to appear.

By this time, Dylan and Baez were prominent in the civil rights movement, singing together at the March on Washington, on August 28, 1963. Dylan's third album, The Times They Are a-Changin', reflected a more politicized and cynical Dylan. The songs often took as their subject matter contemporary stories, with "Only a Pawn in Their Game," addressing the murder of civil rights worker Medgar Evers, followed by the Brechtian "The Lonesome Death of Hattie Carroll," concerning the death of black hotel barmaid Hattie Carroll, at the hands of young white socialite William Zantzinger.

On a more general theme, "Ballad of Hollis Brown" and "North Country Blues," addressed despair engendered by the breakdown of farming and mining communities. This political material was accompanied by two personal love songs, "Boots of Spanish Leather" and "One Too Many Mornings". During the Nashville Skyline sessions in 1969, Dylan and Johnny Cash recorded a duet of the song, which was not released.

By the end of 1963, Dylan felt both manipulated and constrained by the folk and protest movements. Accepting the "Tom Paine Award," from the National Emergency Civil Liberties Committee, shortly after the assassination of John F. Kennedy, an intoxicated Dylan questioned the role of the committee, characterized the members as old and balding then claimed to see something of himself and of every man, in Kennedy's alleged assassin, Lee Harvey Oswald.

Another Side of Bob Dylan, recorded on a single evening in June 1964, had a lighter mood, with the humorous Dylan reemerging on "I Shall Be Free No. 10" and "Motorpsycho Nightmare". "Spanish Harlem Incident" and "To Ramona" were passionate love songs, while "Black Crow Blues" and "I Don't Believe You (She Acts Like We Never Have Met)," suggested the rock and roll, soon to dominate Dylan's music.

"It Ain't Me Babe", on the surface a song about spurned love, has been described as a rejection of the role of political spokesman thrust upon him. His newest direction was signaled by two lengthy songs: the impressionistic "Chimes of Freedom", which set social commentary against a metaphorical landscape, in a style characterized by Allen Ginsberg as, "chains of flashing images," and "My Back Pages", which attacked the simplistic and arch seriousness of his own earlier topical songs, seeming to predict the backlash he was about to encounter from his former champions.

In the latter half of 1964 and 1965, Dylan moved from folk songwriter to folk-rock, pop-music star, with his jeans and work shirts being replaced by a Carnaby Street wardrobe, sunglasses day or night, and pointed "Beatle boots". A London reporter wrote: "Hair that would set the teeth of a comb on edge. A loud shirt that would dim the neon lights of Leicester Square. He looks like an undernourished cockatoo." Dylan began to spar with interviewers, as appearing on the Les Crane television show, when asked about a movie he planned, he told Crane it would be a cowboy horror movie. Asked if he played the cowboy, Dylan replied, "No, I play my mother."

Dylan's late March 1965 album Bringing It All Back Home was another leap, featuring his first recordings with electric instruments. The first single, "Subterranean Homesick Blues", owed much to Chuck Berry's "Too Much Monkey Business", its free association lyrics described as harkening back to the energy of beat poetry, being a forerunner of rap and hip-hop.

The song was provided with an early film clip, which opened D. A. Pennebaker's cinéma vérité presentation, of Dylan's 1965 tour of Great Britain, Dont Look Back. Instead of miming, Dylan illustrated the lyrics, by throwing cue cards, containing key words from the song on the ground. Pennebaker said the sequence was Dylan's idea, it having been imitated in music videos and advertisements.

The second side of Bringing It All Back Home contained four long songs, on which Dylan accompanied himself on acoustic guitar and harmonica. "Mr. Tambourine Man" became one of his best known songs, when the Byrds recorded an electric version that reached # 1 in the US and UK ."It's All Over Now, Baby Blue" and "It's Alright Ma (I'm Only Bleeding)," were two of Dylan's key compositions.

In 1965, headlining the Newport Folk Festival, Dylan performed his first electric set since high school, with a pickup group, featuring Mike Bloomfield on guitar and Al Kooper on organ. Dylan had appeared at Newport in 1963 and 1964, but in 1965 met with jeering and booing, leaving the stage after three songs.

The boos were believed to have been from folk fans, whom Dylan had alienated by appearing, unexpectedly, with an electric guitar. Murray Lerner, who filmed the performance, said: "I absolutely think that they were booing Dylan going electric." An alternative account claimed audience members were upset by poor sound and a short set, which was supported by Kooper and one of the directors of the festival, who said his recording proved the only boos were in reaction to the MC's announcement that there was only enough time for a short set.

However, Dylan's performance provoked a hostile response from the folk music establishment. In the September issue of Sing Out!, Ewan MacColl wrote: "Our traditional songs and ballads are the creations of extraordinarily talented artists, working inside disciplines formulated over time ...' but what of Bobby Dylan?' scream the outraged teenagers ... Only a completely non-critical audience, nourished on the watery pap of pop music, could have fallen for such tenth-rate drivel."

On July 29, four days after Newport, Dylan was back in the studio in New York, recording "Positively 4th Street". The lyrics contained images of vengeance and paranoia, which has been interpreted as Dylan's put-down of former friends from the folk community—friends he had known in clubs along West 4th Street.

In July 1965, the single "Like a Rolling Stone" peaked at # 2 in the U.S. and at # 4 in the UK charts. At over six minutes in duration, the song altered what a pop single could convey. Bruce Springsteen, in his speech for Dylan's inauguration into the Rock and Roll Hall of Fame, said that on first hearing the single, "that snare shot sounded like somebody'd kicked open the door to your mind".

In 2004 then 2011, Rolling Stone listed it as # 1 of "The 500 Greatest Songs of All Time". The song opened Dylan's next album, Highway 61 Revisited, named after the road that led from Dylan's Minnesota to the musical hotbed of New Orleans. The songs were in the same vein as the hit single, flavoured by Mike Bloomfield's blues guitar and Al Kooper's organ riffs.

"Desolation Row", backed by acoustic guitar and understated bass, offered the sole exception, with Dylan alluding to figures in Western culture, in a song described by Andy Gill as "an 11-minute epic of entropy, which takes the form of a Fellini-esque parade of grotesques and oddities, featuring a huge cast of celebrated characters, some historical (Einstein, Nero), some biblical (Noah, Cain and Abel), some fictional (Ophelia, Romeo, Cinderella), some literary (T.S. Eliot and Ezra Pound), and some who fit into none of the above categories, notably Dr. Filth and his dubious nurse."

In support of the album, Dylan was booked for two U.S. concerts with Al Kooper and Harvey Brooks from his studio crew and Robbie Robertson and Levon Helm, former members of Ronnie Hawkins's backing band the Hawks.[107] On August 28 at Forest Hills Tennis Stadium, the group was heckled by an audience still annoyed by Dylan's electric sound. The band's reception on September 3 at the Hollywood Bowl was more favorable.[108]

From September 24, 1965, in Austin, Texas, Dylan toured the U.S. and Canada for six months, backed by five musicians from the Hawks, who became known as the Band. While Dylan and the Hawks met increasingly receptive audiences, their studio efforts floundered. Producer Bob Johnston persuaded Dylan to record in Nashville in February 1966, surrounding him with top-notch session men, with Robertson and Kooper coming from New York City to play on the sessions, at Dylan's insistence.

The Nashville sessions produced the double album Blonde on Blonde (1966), featuring what Dylan called "that thin, wild mercury sound". Kooper described it as "taking two cultures and smashing them together, with a huge explosion": the musical world of Nashville and the world of the "quintessential New York hipster," Bob Dylan.

On November 22, 1965, Dylan secretly married 25-year-old former model Sara Lownds. Robertson wrote in his memoir, about receiving a phone call that morning to accompany the couple to the court then later to a reception hosted by Al Grossman, at the Algonquin Hotel.

Some of Dylan's friends, including Ramblin' Jack Elliott, said that immediately after the event, Dylan denied he was married. Journalist Nora Ephron made the news public in the New York Post in February 1966, with the headline "Hush! Bob Dylan is wed."

Dylan toured Australia and Europe in April and May 1966, each show being split in two. Dylan performed solo during the first half, accompanying himself on acoustic guitar and harmonica then in the second, backed by the Hawks, he played electrically amplified music. This contrast provoked many fans into jeering and slow handclapping.

The tour culminated in a raucous confrontation between Dylan and his audience, at the Manchester Free Trade Hall, in England, on May 17, 1966. A recording of this concert was released in 1998: The Bootleg Series Vol. 4: Bob Dylan Live 1966. At the climax of the evening, a member of the audience, angered by Dylan's electric backing, shouted: "Judas!" to which Dylan responded, "I don't believe you ... You're a liar!" He then turned to his band to say, "Play it fucking loud!" as they launched into the final song of the night—"Like a Rolling Stone".

During his 1966 tour, Dylan was described as exhausted, acting "as if on a death trip". D. A. Pennebaker, the film maker accompanying the tour, described Dylan as "taking a lot of amphetamine and who-knows-what-else." In a 1969 interview with Jann Wenner, Dylan said, "I was on the road for almost five years. It wore me down. I was on drugs, a lot of things ... just to keep going, you know?"

In 2011, BBC Radio 4 reported that in an interview that Robert Shelton taped in 1966, Dylan had said he'd kicked heroin in New York City: "I got very, very strung out for a while ... I had about a $25-a-day habit and I kicked it." Some journalists questioned the validity of this confession, pointing out that Dylan had "been telling journalists wild lies about his past, since the earliest days of his career."

After his tour, Dylan returned to New York, but the pressures increased, with ABC Television having paid an advance for a TV show, his publisher, Macmillan, demanding a manuscript of the poem/novel Tarantula and his manager, Albert Grossman having scheduled a concert tour for the latter part of the year.

On July 29, 1966, Dylan crashed his 500cc Triumph Tiger 100 motorcycle, near his home in Woodstock, New York, being thrown to the ground. Though the extent of his injuries was never fully disclosed, Dylan said that he broke several vertebrae in his neck. Mystery still surrounds the circumstances of the accident, as no ambulance was called to the scene and Dylan was not hospitalized.

Dylan's biographers have written that the crash offered Dylan the chance to escape the pressures around him, Dylan having confirmed this interpretation in his autobiography: "I had been in a motorcycle accident and I'd been hurt, but I recovered. Truth was that I wanted to get out of the rat race." Dylan withdrew from public, apart from a few appearances, not touring again for almost eight years.

Once Dylan was well enough to resume creative work, he began to edit D. A. Pennebaker's film of his 1966 tour, a rough cut being shown to ABC Television but rejected as incomprehensible to a mainstream audience. The film was subsequently titled Eat the Document on bootleg copies, having been screened at a handful of film festivals.

In 1967 he began recording with the Hawks at his home and in the basement of the Hawks' nearby house, "Big Pink". These songs, initially demos for other artists to record, provided hits for Julie Driscoll and the Brian Auger Trinity ("This Wheel's on Fire"), The Byrds ("You Ain't Goin' Nowhere", "Nothing Was Delivered"), and Manfred Mann ("Mighty Quinn").

Columbia released selections in 1975, as The Basement Tapes, over the years, more songs recorded by Dylan and his band in 1967 having appeared on bootleg recordings, culminating in a five-CD set titled The Genuine Basement Tapes, containing 107 songs and alternative takes. In the coming months, the Hawks recorded the album Music from Big Pink, using songs they worked on in their basement in Woodstock then renamed themselves the Band, beginning a long recording and performing career of their own.

In October and November 1967, Dylan returned to Nashville, back in the studio after 19 months, being accompanied by Charlie McCoy on bass, Kenny Buttrey on drums, and Pete Drake on steel guitar. The result was John Wesley Harding, a contemplative record of shorter songs, set in a landscape that drew on the American West and the Bible.

The sparse structure and instrumentation, with lyrics that took the Judeo-Christian tradition seriously, departed from Dylan's earlier work and from the psychedelic fervor of the 1960s. It included "All Along the Watchtower", with lyrics derived from the Book of Isaiah (21:5–9), the song later being recorded by Jimi Hendrix, whose version Dylan acknowledged as definitive. Woody Guthrie died on October 3, 1967, Dylan making his first live appearance in twenty months, at a Guthrie memorial concert, held at Carnegie Hall on January 20, 1968, where he was backed by the Band.

Dylan's next release, Nashville Skyline (1969), was mainstream country, featuring Nashville musicians, a mellow-voiced Dylan, a duet with Johnny Cash, and the hit single "Lay Lady Lay". Variety wrote, "Dylan is definitely doing something that can be called singing. Somehow he has managed to add an octave to his range." During one recording session, Dylan and Cash recorded a series of duets but only their version of Dylan's "Girl from the North Country" was released on the album.

In May 1969, Dylan appeared on the first episode of Johnny Cash's television show, singing a duet with Cash of "Girl from the North Country", with solos of "Living the Blues" and "I Threw It

All Away". Dylan then traveled to England, to top the bill at the Isle of Wight festival, on August 31, 1969, after rejecting overtures to appear at the Woodstock Festival.

In the early 1970s, critics argued that Dylan's output was varied and unpredictable. Rolling Stone writer Greil Marcus asked "What is this shit?" on first listening to Self Portrait, released in June 1970, a double LP including few original songs, which was poorly received. In October 1970, Dylan released New Morning, considered a return to form, including "Day of the Locusts", a song in which Dylan gave an account of receiving an honorary degree from Princeton University on June 9, 1970.

In November 1968, Dylan had co-written "I'd Have You Anytime" with George Harrison, who'd recorded it, with Dylan's "If Not for You," for his 1970 solo triple album, All Things Must Pass. Dylan's surprise appearance at Harrison's 1971 Concert for Bangladesh, attracted media coverage, as his live appearances had become rare.

Between March 16 and 19, 1971, Dylan reserved three days at Blue Rock, a small studio in Greenwich Village, to record with Leon Russell, the sessions resulting in "Watching the River Flow" and a new recording of "When I Paint My Masterpiece". On November 4, 1971, Dylan recorded "George Jackson", the single being a surprising return to protest material, mourning the killing of Black Panther George Jackson in San Quentin State Prison that year. Dylan contributed piano and harmony to Steve Goodman's album, Somebody Else's Troubles, under the pseudonym Robert Milkwood Thomas, derived from the play Under Milk Wood by Dylan Thomas and his own previous name, in September 1972.

That year Dylan signed to appear in Sam Peckinpah's film Pat Garrett and Billy the Kid, providing songs and backing music for the movie, and playing "Alias", a member of Billy's gang with some historical basis. Despite the film's failure at the box office, the song "Knockin' on Heaven's Door" became one of Dylan's most covered songs.

Also in 1972, Dylan protested against the move to deport John Lennon and Yoko Ono, who had been convicted of possessing cannabis, by sending a letter to the U.S. Immigration Service, in part: "Hurray for John & Yoko. Let them stay and live here and breathe. The country's got plenty of room and space. Let John and Yoko stay!"

Dylan began 1973 by signing with a new label, David Geffen's Asylum Records and Island in the UK, when his contract with Columbia Records expired. On his next album, Planet Waves, he used the Band as his backing group, while rehearsing for a tour, it including two versions of "Forever Young", which became one of his most popular songs. As one critic described it, the song projected "something hymnal and heartfelt that spoke of the father in Dylan", who said: "I wrote it thinking about one of my boys and not wanting to be too sentimental."

Columbia Records simultaneously released 'Dylan', a collection of studio outtakes, almost exclusively covers, widely interpreted as a churlish response to Dylan's signing with a rival record label. In January 1974, Dylan returned to touring after seven years, backed by the Band, embarking on a North American tour of 40 concerts.

A live double album, Before the Flood, was released on Asylum Records, with Clive Davis stating that Columbia Records had sent word that they "will spare nothing to bring Dylan back into the fold". Dylan had second thoughts about Asylum, miffed that while there had been millions of unfulfilled ticket requests for the 1974 tour, Geffen had sold only 700,000 copies of Planet Waves, so he returned to Columbia Records, which reissued his two Asylum albums.

After the tour, Dylan and his wife became estranged. He filled a small red notebook with songs about relationships and ruptures then recorded an album entitled Blood on the Tracks in September 1974. Dylan delayed the release, re-recording half the songs at Sound 80 Studios in Minneapolis, with production assistance from his brother, David Zimmerman.

Released in early 1975, Blood on the Tracks received mixed reviews. In the NME, Nick Kent described "the accompaniments [as] often so trashy they sound like mere practice takes." In Rolling Stone, Jon Landau wrote that "the record has been made with typical shoddiness." However, over the years critics came to see it as one of Dylan's greatest achievements.

In Salon.com, Bill Wyman wrote: "Blood on the Tracks is his only flawless album and his best produced; the songs, each of them, are constructed in disciplined fashion. It is his kindest album and most dismayed, and seems in hindsight to have achieved a sublime balance between the logorrhea-plagued excesses of his mid-1960s output and the self-consciously simple compositions of his post-accident years." Novelist Rick Moody called it "the truest, most honest account of a love affair from tip to stern, ever put down on magnetic tape."

Dylan said of Tangled Up in Blue, the opening song from Blood on the Tracks: "I was trying to deal with the concept of time, and the way the characters change from the first person to the third person, and you're never sure if the first person is talking or the third person but as you look at the whole thing it really doesn't matter."

In the middle of that year, Dylan wrote a ballad championing boxer Rubin "Hurricane" Carter, imprisoned for a triple murder in Paterson, New Jersey, in 1966. After visiting Carter in jail, Dylan wrote "Hurricane", presenting the case for Carter's innocence. Despite its length—over eight minutes—the song was released as a single, peaking at # 33 on the U.S. Billboard chart, being performed at every 1975 date of Dylan's next tour, the Rolling Thunder Revue.

The tour featured about one hundred performers and supporters from the Greenwich Village folk scene, including T-Bone Burnett, Ramblin' Jack Elliott, Joni Mitchell, David Mansfield, Roger McGuinn, Mick Ronson, Joan Baez, and Scarlet Rivera, whom Dylan discovered walking down the street, her violin case on her back. Allen Ginsberg accompanied the troupe, staging scenes for the film Dylan was shooting. Sam Shepard was hired to write the screenplay, but ended up accompanying the tour as informal chronicler.

Running through late 1975 then again through early 1976, the tour encompassed the release of the album Desire, with many of Dylan's new songs featuring a travelogue-like narrative style, showing the influence of his new collaborator, playwright Jacques Levy. The 1976 half of the tour was documented by a TV concert special, Hard Rain, with the LP of the same name, no concert album from the better-received and better-known opening half of the tour having been released until 2002's Live 1975.

The 1975 tour with the Revue, provided the backdrop to Dylan's nearly four-hour film Renaldo and Clara, a sprawling narrative, mixed with concert footage and reminiscences. Released in 1978, the movie received poor, sometimes scathing, reviews. Later in that year, a two-hour edit, dominated by the concert performances, was more widely released.

In November 1976, Dylan appeared at the Band's "farewell" concert, with Eric Clapton, Joni Mitchell, Muddy Waters, Van Morrison and Neil Young. Martin Scorsese's cinematic chronicle, The Last Waltz, in 1978, included about half of Dylan's set. In 1976, Dylan wrote and duetted on "Sign Language," for Eric Clapton's No Reason To Cry.

In 1978, Dylan embarked on a year-long world tour, performing 114 shows in Japan, the Far East, Europe and the US, to a total audience of two million, having assembled an eight-piece band, with three backing singers. Concerts in Tokyo in February and March were released as the live double album, Bob Dylan At Budokan.

Reviews were mixed, Robert Christgau awarding the album a C+ rating, with a derisory review, while Janet Maslin defended it in Rolling Stone, writing: "These latest live versions of his old songs, have the effect of liberating Bob Dylan from the originals." When Dylan brought the tour to the U.S. in September 1978, the press described the look and sound as a 'Las Vegas Tour'. The 1978 tour grossed more than $20 million, Dylan telling the Los Angeles Times that he had debts, because "I had a couple of bad years. I put a lot of money into the movie, built a big house ... and it costs a lot to get divorced in California."

In April and May 1978, Dylan took the same band and vocalists into Rundown Studios in Santa Monica, California, to record an album of new material: Street-Legal. It was described by Michael Gray as, "after Blood On The Tracks, arguably Dylan's best record of the 1970s: a crucial album, documenting a crucial period in Dylan's own life". However, it had poor sound and mixing, attributed to Dylan's studio practices, muddying the instrumental detail, until a remastered CD release in 1999 restored some of the songs' strengths.

In the late 1970s, Dylan converted to Evangelical Christianity, undertaking a three month discipleship course, run by the Association of Vineyard Churches then released two albums of contemporary gospel music. Slow Train Coming (1979) featured the guitar accompaniment of Mark Knopfler of Dire Straits, being produced by veteran R&B producer Jerry Wexler, who said that Dylan had tried to evangelize him during the recording. He'd replied: "Bob, you're dealing with a 62-year-old Jewish atheist. Let's just make an album."

Dylan won the Grammy Award for Best Male Rock Vocal Performance for the song "Gotta Serve Somebody", with the album reaching No. 3 on the U.S. Billboard 200 chart, His second Christian-themed album, Saved (1980), received mixed reviews, having been described by Michael Gray as "the nearest thing to a follow-up album Dylan has ever made, Slow Train Coming II and inferior." When touring in late 1979 then early 1980, Dylan would not play his older, secular works, delivering declarations of his faith from the stage, such as:

"Years ago they ... said I was a prophet. I used to say, "No I'm not a prophet" they say "Yes you are, you're a prophet." I said, "No it's not me." They used to say "You sure are a prophet." They used to convince me I was a prophet. Now I come out and say Jesus Christ is the answer. They say, 'Bob Dylan's no prophet.' They just can't handle it."

Dylan's Christianity was unpopular with some fans and musicians, shortly before his murder, John Lennon recording "Serve Yourself," in response to Dylan's "Gotta Serve Somebody". By 1981, Stephen Holden wrote in the New York Times that "neither age (he's now 40) nor his much-publicized conversion to born-again Christianity, has altered his essentially iconoclastic temperament."

In late 1980, Dylan briefly played concerts billed as "A Musical Retrospective", restoring popular 1960s songs to the repertoire. Shot of Love, recorded early the next year, featured his first secular compositions in more than two years, mixed with Christian songs, "Every Grain of Sand," reminding some of William Blake's verses.

In the 1980s, reception of Dylan's recordings varied, from the well-regarded Infidels in 1983, to the panned Down in the Groove in 1988. Michael Gray condemned Dylan's 1980s albums for carelessness in the studio and for failing to release his best songs, Infidels recording sessions, again employing Knopfler on lead guitar and as the album's producer, having resulted in several notable songs that Dylan left off the album. Best regarded of these were "Blind Willie McTell", a tribute to the dead blues musician and an evocation of African American history, "Foot of Pride" and "Lord Protect My Child". These three songs were released on The Bootleg Series Volumes 1–3 (Rare & Unreleased) 1961–1991.

Between July 1984 and March 1985, Dylan recorded Empire Burlesque. Arthur Baker, who had remixed hits for Bruce Springsteen and Cyndi Lauper, was asked to engineer and mix the album. Baker said he felt he was hired to make Dylan's album sound "a little bit more contemporary".

In 1985 Dylan sang on USA for Africa's famine relief single "We Are the World", also joining Artists United Against Apartheid, providing vocals for their single "Sun City". On July 13, 1985, he appeared at the climax at the Live Aid concert at JFK Stadium, Philadelphia. Backed by Keith Richards and Ronnie Wood, he performed a ragged version of "Hollis Brown", his ballad of rural poverty then said to the worldwide audience exceeding one billion people:

"I hope that some of the money ... maybe they can just take a little bit of it, maybe ... one or two million, maybe ... and use it to pay the mortgages on some of the farms and, the farmers here, owe to the banks." His remarks were widely criticized as inappropriate, but they did inspire Willie Nelson to organize a series of events, Farm Aid, to benefit debt-ridden American farmers.

In April 1986, Dylan made a foray into rap music, adding vocals to the opening verse of "Street Rock", featured on Kurtis Blow's album Kingdom Blow. Dylan's next studio album, Knocked Out Loaded, in July 1986, contained three covers, by Little Junior Parker, Kris Kristofferson and the gospel hymn "Precious Memories", plus three collaborations, with Tom Petty, Sam Shepard and Carole Bayer Sager, with two solo compositions by Dylan.

One reviewer said that "the record follows too many detours to be consistently compelling, and some of those detours wind down roads that are indisputably dead ends. By 1986, such uneven records weren't entirely unexpected by Dylan, but that didn't make them any less frustrating." It was the first Dylan album since Freewheelin' (1963) to fail to make the Top 50 but some critics have since called the 11-minute epic that Dylan co-wrote with Sam Shepard, "Brownsville Girl", a work of genius.

In 1986 and 1987, Dylan toured with Tom Petty and the Heartbreakers, sharing vocals with Petty on several songs each night. Dylan also toured with the Grateful Dead in 1987, resulting in a live album, Dylan & The Dead, which received negative reviews: Allmusic said, "Quite possibly the worst album by either Bob Dylan or the Grateful Dead." Dylan then initiated what came to be called the Never Ending Tour on June 7, 1988, performing with a back-up band featuring guitarist G. E. Smith. Dylan continued to tour with a small, evolving band for the next 20 years.

In 1987, Dylan starred in Richard Marquand's movie Hearts of Fire, in which he played Billy Parker, a washed-up rock star turned chicken farmer, whose teenage lover (Fiona) left him for a jaded English synth-pop sensation, played by Rupert Everett. Dylan contributed two original songs to the soundtrack—"Night After Night", and "I Had a Dream About You, Baby", as well as a cover of John Hiatt's "The Usual". The film was a critical and commercial flop.

Dylan was inducted into the Rock and Roll Hall of Fame in January 1988, with Bruce

Springsteen's introduction declaring, "Bob freed your mind, the way Elvis freed your body. He showed us that just because music was innately physical, did not mean that it was anti-intellectual."

The album Down in the Groove, in May 1988, sold even less successfully than his previous studio album. Michael Gray wrote: "The very title undercuts any idea that inspired work may lie within. Here was a further devaluing of the notion of a new Bob Dylan album as something significant."

The critical and commercial disappointment of that album was swiftly followed by the success of the Traveling Wilburys. Dylan co-founded the band with George Harrison, Jeff Lynne, Roy Orbison, and Tom Petty, in late 1988 their multi-platinum Traveling Wilburys Vol. 1, reaching # 3 on the US album chart, featuring songs that were described as Dylan's most accessible compositions in years. Despite Orbison's death in December 1988, the remaining four recorded a second album in May 1990, with the title Traveling Wilburys Vol. 3.

Dylan finished the decade on a critical high note, with Oh Mercy, produced by Daniel Lanois. Michael Gray wrote that the album was: "Attentively written, vocally distinctive, musically warm, and uncompromisingly professional, this cohesive whole is the nearest thing to a great Bob Dylan album in the 1980s."

The track "Most of the Time", a lost love composition, was later prominently featured in the film High Fidelity, while "What Was It You Wanted?" has been interpreted both as a catechism and a wry comment on the expectations of critics and fans. The religious imagery of "Ring Them Bells," struck some critics as a re-affirmation of faith.

Dylan began the 1990s with Under the Red Sky (1990), an about-face from the serious Oh Mercy, the album containing several apparently simple songs, including the title track and "Wiggle Wiggle". It was dedicated to "Gabby Goo Goo", a nickname for the daughter of Dylan and Carolyn Dennis, Desiree Gabrielle Dennis-Dylan, who was four. Sidemen on the album included George Harrison, Slash from Guns N' Roses, David Crosby, Bruce Hornsby, Stevie Ray Vaughan, and Elton John but despite the line-up, the record received bad reviews, selling poorly.

In 1991, Dylan received a Grammy Lifetime Achievement Award from American actor Jack Nicholson. The event coincided with the start of the first Gulf War against Saddam Hussein, with Dylan performing "Masters of War". Dylan then made a short speech, saying "My daddy once said to me, he said, 'Son, it is possible for you to become so defiled in this world that your own mother and father will abandon you. If that happens, God will believe in your ability to mend your own ways.'" This sentiment was subsequently revealed to be a quote from 19th-century German Jewish intellectual, Rabbi Samson Raphael Hirsch.

Over the next few years Dylan returned to his roots, with two albums covering folk and blues numbers: Good as I Been to You (1992) and World Gone Wrong (1993), featuring interpretations and acoustic guitar work. Many critics and fans commented on the quiet beauty of the song "Lone Pilgrim", written by a 19th-century teacher.

In November 1994 Dylan recorded two live shows for MTV Unplugged, saying his wish to perform traditional songs had been overruled by Sony executives, who'd insisted on hits. The album from it, MTV Unplugged, included "John Brown", an unreleased 1962 song, of how enthusiasm for war ends in mutilation and disillusionment.

Dylan's longtime road manager Victor Maymudes, said that the singer quit drinking alcohol in 1994, feeling that Dylan's sobering up had made him "more introverted and a little less social."

With a collection of songs written while snowed in, on his Minnesota ranch, in January 1997 Dylan booked recording time with Daniel Lanois at Miami's Criteria Studios. The subsequent recording sessions were fraught with musical tension. Before the album's release Dylan was hospitalized with a life-threatening heart infection, pericarditis, brought on by histoplasmosis.

His scheduled European tour was cancelled, but Dylan made a speedy recovery then left the hospital saying, "I really thought I'd be seeing Elvis soon." He was back on the road by mid-year, performing before Pope John Paul II, at the World Eucharistic Conference in Bologna, Italy. The Pope treated the audience of 200,000 people to a homily, based on Dylan's lyric "Blowin' in the Wind".

In September Dylan released the new Lanois-produced album, Time Out of Mind. With its bitter assessment of love and morbid ruminations, Dylan's first collection of original songs in seven years was highly acclaimed. One critic wrote: "the songs themselves are uniformly powerful, adding up to Dylan's best overall collection in years," it winning him his first solo "Album of the Year" Grammy Award.

In December 1997, U.S. President Bill Clinton presented Dylan with a Kennedy Center Honor in the East Room of the White House, paying this tribute: "He probably had more impact on people of my generation than any other creative artist. His voice and lyrics haven't always been easy on the ear, but throughout his career Bob Dylan has never aimed to please. He's disturbed the peace and discomforted the powerful."

In 1999, Dylan embarked on a North American tour with Paul Simon, where each alternated as headline act, with a "middle" section where they performed together, starting on the first of June and ending September 18, the collaboration being generally well-received.

Dylan commenced the 2000s by winning the Polar Music Prize in May 2000 and his first Oscar; his song "Things Have Changed", written for the film Wonder Boys, won an Academy Award in March 2001. The Oscar, or a facsimile, tours with him, presiding over shows perched atop an amplifier. The line "sapphire-tinted skies" echoed the verse of Shelley, while "forty miles of bad road" echoed Duane Eddy's hit single.

Recorded with his touring band, Dylan produced the album "Love and Theft" himself, under the pseudonym Jack Frost, released on September 11, 2001, which was critically well received, earning nominations for several Grammy awards. Critics noted that Dylan was widening his musical palette to include rockabilly, Western swing, jazz, and even lounge ballads. "Love and Theft" generated controversy, when The Wall Street Journal pointed out similarities between the album's lyrics and Japanese author Junichi Saga's book, Confessions of a Yakuza.

In 2003, Dylan revisited the evangelical songs from his Christian period, participanting in the CD project Gotta Serve Somebody: The Gospel Songs of Bob Dylan. That year Dylan also released the film Masked & Anonymous, which he co-wrote with director Larry Charles, under the alias Sergei Petrov. Dylan played the central character in the film, Jack Fate, alongside a cast that included Jeff Bridges, Penélope Cruz and John Goodman. The film polarised critics, many dismissing it as an "incoherent mess" but a few treated it as a serious work of art.

In October 2004, Dylan published the first part of his autobiography, Chronicles: Volume One. Confounding expectations, Dylan devoted three chapters to his first year in New York City in 1961–1962, virtually ignoring the mid-1960s, when his fame was at its height. He also devoted chapters to the albums New Morning (1970) and Oh Mercy (1989). The book reached # 2 on The New York Times' Hardcover Non-Fiction best seller list in December 2004, being nominated for a National Book Award.

No Direction Home, Martin Scorsese's acclaimed film biography of Dylan, was first broadcast on September 26–27, 2005, on BBC Two in the UK and PBS in the US. The documentary focused on the period from Dylan's arrival in New York in 1961, to his motorcycle crash in 1966, featuring interviews with Suze Rotolo, Liam Clancy, Joan Baez, Allen Ginsberg, Pete Seeger, Mavis Staples, and Dylan himself. The film received a Peabody Award in April 2006 and a Columbia-duPont Award in January 2007. The accompanying soundtrack featured unreleased songs from Dylan's early career.

Dylan earned yet another distinction, in a 2007 study of US legal opinions and briefs that found his lyrics were quoted by judges and lawyers more than those of any other songwriter, 186 times versus 74 by the Beatles, who were second. Among those quoting Dylan were US Supreme Court Chief Justice John Roberts and Justice Antonin Scalia, both conservatives. The most widely cited lines included "you don't need a weatherman to know which way the wind blows" from "Subterranean Homesick Blues" and "when you ain't got nothing, you got nothing to lose" from "Like a Rolling Stone"

May 3, 2006, saw the premiere of Dylan's radio presenting career, hosting a weekly radio program, Theme Time Radio Hour, for XM Satellite Radio, with song selections revolving around a chosen theme. Dylan played classic and obscure records from the 1930s to the present day, including contemporary artists as diverse as Blur, Prince, L.L. Cool J and the Streets.

The show was praised by fans and critics as "great radio," Dylan telling stories and making eclectic references with his sardonic humour, while achieving a thematic beauty with his musical choices. In April 2009, Dylan broadcast the 100th show in his radio series; the theme being "Goodbye" with the final record played having been Woody Guthrie's "So Long, It's Been Good to Know Yuh", which led to speculation that Dylan's radio excursion had ended.

On August 29, 2006, Dylan released his Modern Times album. Despite some coarsening of Dylan's voice, with a critic for The Guardian characterizing his singing on the album as "a catarrhal death rattle", most reviewers praised the album, many describing it as the final installment of a successful trilogy, embracing Time Out of Mind and "Love and Theft".

Modern Times entered the U.S. charts at # 1, making it Dylan's first album to reach that position since 1976's Desire. The New York Times published an article exploring similarities between some of Dylan's lyrics in Modern Times and the work of the Civil War poet Henry Timrod.

Nominated for three Grammy Awards, Modern Times won Best Contemporary Folk/Americana Album, Dylan also winning Best Solo Rock Vocal Performance for "Someday Baby". Modern Times was named Album of the Year, 2006, by Rolling Stone magazine, and by Uncut in the UK. On the same day that Modern Times was released, the iTunes Music Store released Bob Dylan: The Collection, a digital box set containing all of his albums, 773 tracks in total, along with 42 rare and unreleased tracks.

In August 2007, the award-winning film biography of Dylan, I'm Not There, written and directed by Todd Haynes, was released—bearing the tagline "inspired by the music and many lives of Bob Dylan". The movie used six different actors to represent different aspects of Dylan's life: Christian Bale, Cate Blanchett, Marcus Carl Franklin, Richard Gere, Heath Ledger and Ben Whishaw.

Dylan's previously unreleased 1967 recording, from which the film took its name, was released for the first time on the film's original soundtrack; all other tracks were covers of Dylan songs, specially recorded for the movie by a diverse range of artists, including Sonic Youth, Eddie

Vedder, Mason Jennings, Stephen Malkmus, Jeff Tweedy, Karen O, Willie Nelson, Cat Power, Richie Havens, and Tom Verlaine.

On October 1, 2007, Columbia Records released the triple CD retrospective album 'Dylan', anthologising his entire career under the Dylan 07 logo. As part of this campaign, Mark Ronson produced a re-mix of Dylan's 1966 tune "Most Likely You Go Your Way and I'll Go Mine", released as a maxi-single, which was the first time Dylan had sanctioned a re-mix of one of his classic recordings.

The sophistication of the Dylan 07 marketing campaign, was a reminder that Dylan's commercial profile had risen considerably since the 1990s. This had first become evident in 2004, when Dylan appeared in a TV advertisement for Victoria's Secret lingerie. Three years later, in October 2007, he participated in a multi-media campaign for the 2008 Cadillac Escalade.

In 2009, he gave the highest profile endorsement of his career, appearing with rapper will.i.am in a Pepsi ad that debuted during the telecast of Super Bowl XLIII. The ad, broadcast to a record audience of 98 million viewers, opened with Dylan singing the first verse of "Forever Young," followed by will.i.am doing a hip hop version of the song's third and final verse.

In October 2008, Columbia released The Bootleg Series Vol. 8 – Tell Tale Signs, as both a two-CD set and a three-CD version, with a 150-page hardcover book. The set contained live performances and outtakes from selected studio albums, from Oh Mercy to Modern Times, with soundtrack contributions and collaborations with David Bromberg and Ralph Stanley.

The pricing of the album—the two-CD set went on sale for $18.99 and the three-CD version for $29.99—led to complaints about "rip-off packaging" from some fans and commentators but the release was widely acclaimed by critics. The abundance of alternative takes and unreleased material, suggested to one reviewer that this volume of old outtakes "feels like a new Bob Dylan record, not only for the astonishing freshness of the material, but also for the incredible sound quality and organic feeling of everything here."

Bob Dylan released his album Together Through Life on April 28, 2009. In a conversation with music journalist Bill Flanagan, published on Dylan's website, Dylan explained the genesis of the record, when French film director Olivier Dahan had asked him to supply a song for his new road movie, My Own Love Song, initially only having intended to record a single track, "Life Is Hard," "the record sort of took its own direction". Nine of the ten songs on the album were credited as co-written by Bob Dylan and Robert Hunter.

The album received largely favourable reviews, although several critics described it as a minor addition to Dylan's canon of work. Andy Gill wrote in The Independent that the record "features Dylan in fairly relaxed, spontaneous mood, content to grab such grooves and sentiments as flit momentarily across his radar. So while it may not contain too many landmark tracks, it's one of the most naturally enjoyable albums you'll hear all year."

In its first week of release, the album reached # 1 on the Billboard 200 chart in the U.S., making Bob Dylan, at 67 years of age, the oldest artist to ever debut at # 1. It also reached # 1 on the UK album chart, 39 years after Dylan's previous UK album chart topper New Morning, Dylan holding the record for the longest gap between solo # 1 albums in the UK chart.

On October 13, 2009, Dylan released a Christmas album, Christmas in the Heart, comprising such Christmas standards as "Little Drummer Boy", "Winter Wonderland" and "Here Comes Santa Claus". Dylan's royalties from the sale of this album would benefit the charities Feeding America in the USA, Crisis in the UK, and the World Food Programme.

The album received generally favourable reviews, with The New Yorker stating that Dylan had welded a pre-rock musical sound to "some of his croakiest vocals in a while", speculating that Dylan's intentions might be ironic: "Dylan has a long and highly publicized history with Christianity; to claim there's not a wink in the childish optimism of 'Here Comes Santa Claus' or 'Winter Wonderland,' is to ignore a half-century of biting satire."

In USA Today, Edna Gundersen pointed out that Dylan was "revisiting yuletide styles popularized by Nat King Cole, Mel Tormé, and the Ray Conniff Singers," concluding that Dylan "couldn't sound more sentimental or sincere". In an interview published in The Big Issue, journalist Bill Flanagan asked Dylan why he had performed the songs in a straightforward style, to which Dylan responded: "There wasn't any other way to play it. These songs are part of my life, just like folk songs. You have to play them straight too."

On October 18, 2010, Dylan released Volume 9 of his Bootleg Series, The Witmark Demos. This comprised 47 demo recordings of songs taped between 1962 and 1964, for Dylan's earliest music publishers: Leeds Music in 1962, and Witmark Music from 1962 to 1964. One reviewer described the set as "a hearty glimpse of young Bob Dylan changing the music business, and the world, one note at a time."

The critical aggregator website Metacritic, awarded the album a Metascore of 86, indicating "universal acclaim". In the same week, Sony Legacy released Bob Dylan: The Original Mono Recordings, a box set that for the first time presented Dylan's eight earliest albums, from Bob Dylan (1962) to John Wesley Harding (1967), in their original mono mix in the CD format. The CDs were housed in miniature facsimiles of the original album covers, replete with original liner notes. The set was accompanied by a booklet featuring an essay by music critic Greil Marcus.

On April 12, 2011, Legacy Recordings released Bob Dylan in Concert – Brandeis University 1963, taped at Brandeis University on May 10, 1963, two weeks prior to the release of The Freewheelin' Bob Dylan. The tape was discovered in the archive of music writer Ralph J.

Gleason, the recording carrying liner notes by Michael Gray, who said it captured Dylan "from way back when Kennedy was President and the Beatles hadn't yet reached America. It reveals him not at any Big Moment but giving a performance like his folk club sets of the period... This is the last live performance we have of Bob Dylan before he becomes a star."

The extent to which his work was studied at an academic level, was demonstrated on Dylan's 70th birthday on May 24, 2011, when three universities organized symposia on his work. The University of Mainz, the University of Vienna, and the University of Bristol, invited literary critics and cultural historians to submit papers on aspects of Dylan's work.

Other events, including tribute bands, discussions and simple singalongs, took place around the world, as reported in The Guardian: "From Moscow to Madrid, Norway to Northampton and Malaysia to his home state of Minnesota, self-confessed 'Bobcats,' will gather today to celebrate the 70th birthday of a giant of popular music."

On October 4, 2011, Dylan's label, Egyptian Records, released an album of previously unheard Hank Williams songs, The Lost Notebooks of Hank Williams. Dylan had helped to curate this project, in which songs unfinished when Williams died in 1953, were completed and recorded by a variety of artists, including Dylan himself, his son Jakob Dylan, Levon Helm, Norah Jones, Jack White, and others.

On May 29, 2012, U.S. President Barack Obama awarded Dylan a Presidential Medal of Freedom, in the White House. At the ceremony, Obama praised Dylan's voice for its "unique gravelly power that redefined not just what music sounded like but the message it carried and how it made people feel".

On September 11, 2012, Dylan released his 35th studio album, Tempest, featuring a tribute to John Lennon, "Roll On John", the title track being a 14 minute song about the sinking of the Titanic. Reviewing Tempest for Rolling Stone, Will Hermes gave the album five out of five stars, writing:

"Lyrically, Dylan is at the top of his game, joking around, dropping wordplay and allegories that evade pat readings and quoting other folks' words like a freestyle rapper on fire." Hermes called Tempest "one of [Dylan's] weirdest albums ever", opining, "It may also be the single darkest record in Dylan's catalog." The critical aggregator website Metacritic awarded the album a score of 83 out of 100, indicating "universal acclaim".

On August 27, 2013, Columbia Records released Volume 10 of Dylan's Bootleg Series, Another Self Portrait (1969–1971). The album contained 35 previously unreleased tracks, including alternate takes and demos from Dylan's 1969–1971 recording sessions, during the making of the Self Portrait and New Morning albums.

The box set also included a live recording of Dylan's performance with the Band, at the Isle of Wight Festival in 1969. Another Self Portrait received favourable reviews, earning a score of 81 on the critical aggregator, Metacritic, indicating "universal acclaim". AllMusic critic Thom Jurek wrote, "For fans, this is more than a curiosity, it's an indispensable addition to the catalog."

On November 4, 2013, Columbia Records released Bob Dylan: Complete Album Collection: Vol. One, a boxed set containing all 35 of Dylan's studio albums, six albums of live recordings, and a collection, entitled Sidetracks, of singles, songs from films and non-album material. The box included new album-by-album liner notes, written by Clinton Heylin with an introduction by Bill Flanagan.

On the same date, Columbia released a compilation, The Very Best of Bob Dylan, which was available in both single CD and double CD formats. To publicize the 35 album box set, an innovative video of the song "Like a Rolling Stone" was released on Dylan's website. The interactive video, created by director Vania Heymann, allowed viewers to switch between 16 simulated TV channels, all featuring characters who were lip-synching the lyrics of the 48-year-old song.

On February 2, 2014, Dylan appeared in a commercial for the Chrysler 200 car, which was screened during the 2014 Super Bowl American football game. At the end of the commercial, Dylan said: "So let Germany brew your beer, let Switzerland make your watch, let Asia assemble your phone. We will build your car." Dylan's Super Bowl commercial generated controversy and op-ed pieces, discussing the protectionist implications of his words, and whether the singer had "sold out" to corporate interests.

In 2013 and 2014, auction house sales demonstrated the high cultural value attached to Dylan's mid-1960s work, and the record prices that collectors were willing to pay for artefacts from this period. In December 2013, the Fender Stratocaster which Dylan had played at the 1965 Newport Folk Festival fetched $965,000, the second highest price paid for a guitar. In June 2014, Dylan's hand-written lyrics of "Like a Rolling Stone", his 1965 hit single, fetched $2 million dollars at auction, a record for a popular music manuscript.

On October 28, 2014, Simon & Schuster published a massive 960 page, thirteen and a half pound edition of Dylan's lyrics, The Lyrics: Since 1962. The book was edited by literary critic Christopher Ricks, Julie Nemrow and Lisa Nemrow, to offer variant versions of Dylan's songs, sourced from out-takes and live performances. A limited edition of 50 books, signed by Dylan, was priced at $5,000. "It's the biggest, most expensive book we've ever published, as far as I know," said Jonathan Karp, Simon & Schuster's president and publisher.

On November 4, 2014, Columbia Records/Legacy Recordings released The Basement Tapes

Complete by Bob Dylan and the Band. These 138 tracks, in a six-CD box formed Volume 11 of Dylan's Bootleg Series. The 1975 album, The Basement Tapes, contained some of the songs which Dylan and the Band recorded in their homes in Woodstock, New York, in 1967. Subsequently, over 100 recordings and alternate takes had circulated on bootleg records. The sleeve notes for the new box set were by Sid Griffin, American musician and author of Million Dollar Bash: Bob Dylan, the Band, and the Basement Tapes.

On February 3, 2015, Dylan released Shadows in the Night, featuring ten songs written between 1923 and 1963, which have been described as part of the Great American Songbook. All the songs on the album were recorded by Frank Sinatra but both critics and Dylan himself cautioned against seeing the record as a collection of "Sinatra covers".

Dylan explained, "I don't see myself as covering these songs in any way. They've been covered enough. Buried, as a matter of fact. What me and my band are basically doing is uncovering them. Lifting them out of the grave and bringing them into the light of day." In an interview, Dylan said he had been thinking about making this record since hearing Willie Nelson's 1978 album Stardust.

Shadows In the Night received favourable reviews, scoring 82 on the critical aggregator Metacritic. Critics praised the restrained instrumental backings and Dylan's singing, saying that the material had elicited his best vocal performances in recent years. Bill Prince in GQ commented:

"A performer who's had to hear his influence, in virtually every white pop recording made since he debuted his own self-titled album back in 1962, imagines himself into the songs of his pre-rock'n'roll early youth." In The Independent, Andy Gill wrote that the recordings "have a lingering, languid charm, which... help to liberate the material from the rusting manacles of big-band and cabaret mannerisms." The album debuted at # 1 in the UK Albums Chart, in its first week of release.

On October 5, 2015, IBM launched a marketing campaign for its Watson computer system, featuring Dylan, who was seen conversing with the computer, which said it had read all his lyrics and reports: "My analysis shows that your major themes are that time passes and love fades." Dylan replied: "That sounds about right."

On November 6, 2015, Sony Music released The Bootleg Series Vol. 12: The Cutting Edge 1965–1966. This work comprised previously unreleased material from the three albums 'Dylan' recorded between January 1965 and March 1966: Bringing It All Back Home, Highway 61 Revisited and Blonde on Blonde.

The records were released in three formats: a 2-CD "Best Of" version, a 6-CD "Deluxe edition", and an 18-CD "Collector's Edition," in a limited edition of 5,000 units. On Dylan's website the

"Collector's Edition" was described as containing "every single note recorded by Bob Dylan in the studio in 1965/1966". The critical aggregator website Metacritic awarded Cutting Edge a score of 99. The Best of the Cutting Edge entered the Billboard Top Rock Albums chart at # 1 on November 18, based on its first-week sales.

On March 2, 2016, it was announced that Dylan had sold an extensive archive of about 6,000 items, to the George Kaiser Family Foundation and the University of Tulsa. It was reported that the sale price was "an estimated $15 million to $20 million", the archive comprising notebooks, drafts of Dylan lyrics, recordings, and correspondence.

Filmed material in the collection included 30 hours of outtakes from the 1965 tour documentary Dont Look Back, 30 hours of footage shot on Dylan's legendary 1966 electric tour, and 50 hours shot on the 1975 Rolling Thunder Revue. The archive was housed at the Helmerich Center for American Research, a facility at the Gilcrease Museum.

On May 20, Dylan released Fallen Angels, which was described as "a direct continuation of the work of 'uncovering' the Great Songbook that he began on last year's Shadows In the Night." The album contained twelve songs by classic songwriters such as Harold Arlen, Sammy Cahn and Johnny Mercer, eleven of which had been recorded by Sinatra.

Jim Farber wrote in Entertainment Weekly: "Tellingly, [Dylan] delivers these songs of love lost and cherished, not with a burning passion but with the wistfulness of experience. They're memory songs now, intoned with a present sense of commitment. Released just four days ahead of his 75th birthday, they couldn't be more age-appropriate." The album received a score of 79 on critical aggregator website Metacritic, denoting "generally favourable reviews".

On October 13th, '16, the Nobel Prize committee announced it had awarded Dylan the Nobel Prize in Literature "for having created new poetic expressions within the great American song tradition".

On November 11, 2016, Legacy Recordings released a 36-CD set, The 1966 Live Recordings, including every known recording of Bob Dylan's 1966 concert tour. Legacy Recordings president Adam Block said: "While doing the archival research for The Cutting Edge 1965–1966, last year's box set of Dylan's mid-'60s studio sessions, we were continually struck by how great his 1966 live recordings really are."

The recordings commenced with the concert in White Plains, New York on February 5, 1966, ending with the Royal Albert Hall concert in London on May 27. The liner notes for the set were by Clinton Heylin, author of the book, Judas!: From Forest Hills to the Free Trade Hall: A Historical View of Dylan's Big Boo, a study of the 1966 tour. The New York Times stated that most of the concerts had "never been heard in any form", describing the set as "a monumental addition to the corpus".

On March 31, 2017, Dylan released his triple album, Triplicate, comprising 30 new recordings of classic American songs, including "As Time Goes By" by Herman Hupfeld and "Stormy Weather" by Harold Arlen and Ted Koehler. Dylan's 38th studio album was recorded in Hollywood's Capitol Studios, featuring his touring band.

Dylan posted a long interview on his website to promote the album then was asked if this material was an exercise in nostalgia. "Nostalgic? No I wouldn't say that. It's not taking a trip down memory lane or longing and yearning for the good old days or fond memories of what's no more. A song like "Sentimental Journey" is not a way back when song, it doesn't emulate the past, it's attainable and down to earth, it's in the here and now."

The album was awarded a score of 84 on critical aggregator website Metacritic, critics praising the thoroughness of Dylan's exploration of the great American songbook, though, in the opinion of Uncut: "For all its easy charms, Triplicate labours its point to the brink of overkill. After five albums' worth of croon toons, this feels like a fat full stop on a fascinating chapter."

Conor McPherson's play, Girl from the North Country, where dramatic action was broken up by 20 Dylan songs, opened in London's The Old Vic on July 26, 2017. The project had begun when Dylan's office approached McPherson, suggesting creating a play using Dylan songs. The drama received favourable reviews.

On September 20, 2017, the song "When You Gonna Wake Up (Oslo, Norway - July 9, 1981)" was published on Dylan's VEVO Youtube. The song was taken from the forthcoming The Bootleg Series Vol. 13: Trouble No More 1979–1981, consisting of 8 CDs and 1 DVD, scheduled for release on November 3, 2017. Trouble No More documents what Rolling Stone described as Dylan's "Born Again Christian period of 1979 to 1981 - an intense, wildly controversial time that produced three albums and some of the most confrontational concerts of his long career."

The Never Ending Tour commenced on June 7, 1988, Dylan having played roughly 100 dates a year for the entirety of the 1990s and 2000s—a heavier schedule than most performers who started out in the 1960s. By May 2013, Dylan and his band had played more than 2,500 shows, anchored by long-time bassist Tony Garnier, drummer George Recile, multi-instrumentalist Donnie Herron, and guitarist Charlie Sexton.

To the dismay of some of his audience, Dylan's performances remained unpredictable as he altered his arrangements and changed his vocal approach, night after night. Critical opinion on Dylan's shows remained divided, critics such as Richard Williams and Andy Gill having argued that Dylan had found a successful way to present his rich legacy of material. Others had criticized his live performances, for mangling and spitting out "the greatest lyrics ever written, so that they are effectively unrecognisable", and giving so little to the audience that "it is difficult to understand what he is doing on stage at all."

Dylan's performances in China in April 2011 generated controversy, some criticising him for not making any explicit comment on the political situation in China, and for allegedly allowing the Chinese authorities to censor his set list. Others defended Dylan's performances, arguing that such criticism represented a misunderstanding of Dylan's art, and that no evidence for the censorship of Dylan's set list existed.

In response to these allegations, Dylan posted a statement on his website: "As far as censorship goes, the Chinese government had asked for the names of the songs that I would be playing. There's no logical answer to that, so we sent them the set lists from the previous 3 months. If there were any songs, verses or lines censored, nobody ever told me about it and we played all the songs that we intended to play."

At the beginning of 2017, Dylan announced his forthcoming tour of Europe, commencing in Stockholm on April 1, and ending in Dublin on May 11. In June and July, Dylan's tour continued across Canada and the US.

The cover of Dylan's album Self Portrait (1970), is a reproduction of a painting of a face by Dylan, another of his paintings having been reproduced on the cover of the 1974 album Planet Waves. In 1994 Random House published Drawn Blank, a book of Dylan's drawings. In 2007, the first public exhibition of Dylan's paintings, The Drawn Blank Series, opened at the Kunstsammlungen in Chemnitz, Germany, showcasing more than 200 watercolours and gouaches made from the original drawings.

The exhibition coincided with the publication of Bob Dylan: The Drawn Blank Series, which included 170 reproductions from the series. From September 2010 until April 2011, the National Gallery of Denmark exhibited 40 large-scale acrylic paintings by Dylan, The Brazil Series.

In July 2011, a leading contemporary art gallery, Gagosian Gallery, announced their representation of Dylan's paintings. An exhibition of Dylan's art, The Asia Series, opened at the Gagosian Madison Avenue Gallery on September 20, displaying Dylan's paintings of scenes in China and the Far East.

The New York Times reported that "some fans and Dylanologists have raised questions, about whether some of these paintings are based on the singer's own experiences and observations, or on photographs that are widely available and were not taken by Mr. Dylan." The Times pointed to close resemblances between Dylan's paintings and historic photos of Japan and China, and photos taken by Dmitri Kessel and Henri Cartier-Bresson. The Magnum photo agency confirmed that Dylan had licensed the reproduction rights of these photographs.

Dylan's second show at the Gagosian Gallery, Revisionist Art, opened in November 2012. The show consisted of thirty paintings, transforming and satirizing popular magazines, including Playboy and Babytalk. In February 2013, Dylan exhibited the New Orleans Series of paintings at the Palazzo Reale in Milan. In August 2013, Britain's National Portrait Gallery in London, hosted Dylan's first major UK exhibition, Face Value, featuring twelve pastel portraits.

In November 2013, the Halcyon Gallery in London mounted Mood Swings, an exhibition in which Dylan displayed seven wrought iron gates he had made. In a statement released by the gallery, Dylan said, "I've been around iron all my life, ever since I was a kid. I was born and raised in iron ore country, where you could breathe it and smell it every day. Gates appeal to me because of the negative space they allow. They can be closed but at the same time they allow the seasons and breezes to enter and flow. They can shut you out or shut you in and in some ways there is no difference."

In November 2016, the Halcyon Gallery featured a collection of drawings, watercolours and acrylic works by Dylan. The exhibition, The Beaten Path, depicted American landscapes and urban scenes, inspired by Dylan's travels across the USA. The show was well reviewed by Vanity Fair, the Telegraph, and Asia Times Online, being scheduled to tour in 2017. Since 1994, Dylan has published seven books of paintings and drawings.

Discography

Bob Dylan (1962)

The Freewheelin' Bob Dylan (1963)

The Times They Are a-Changin' (1964)

Another Side of Bob Dylan (1964)

Bringing It All Back Home (1965)

Highway 61 Revisited (1965)

Blonde on Blonde (1966)

John Wesley Harding (1967)

Nashville Skyline (1969)

Self Portrait (1970)

New Morning (1970)

Pat Garrett & Billy the Kid (1973)

Dylan (1973)

Planet Waves (1974)

Blood on the Tracks (1975)

The Basement Tapes (1975)

Desire (1976)

Street Legal (1978)

Slow Train Coming (1979)

Saved (1980)

Shot of Love (1981)

Infidels (1983)

Empire Burlesque (1985)

Knocked Out Loaded (1986)

Down in the Groove (1988)

Oh Mercy (1989)

Under the Red Sky (1990)

Good as I Been to You (1992)

World Gone Wrong (1993)

Time Out of Mind (1997)

Love and Theft (2001)

Modern Times (2006)

Together Through Life (2009)

Christmas in the Heart (2009)

Tempest (2012)

Shadows in the Night (2015)

Fallen Angels (2016)

Triplicate (2017)

Dylan has published Tarantula, a work of prose poetry, Chronicles: Volume One, the first part of his memoirs, several books of the lyrics of his songs, and seven books of his art. He has been the subject of many biographies and critical studies.

Dylan's first serious relationship was with artist Suze Rotolo, a daughter of American Communist Party radicals. Dylan said, "She was the most erotic thing I'd ever seen... The air was suddenly filled with banana leaves. We started talking and my head started to spin." Rotolo was photographed, arm-in-arm with Dylan, on the cover of his album The Freewheelin' Bob Dylan.

Critics have connected Rotolo to some of Dylan's early love songs, including "Don't Think Twice It's All Right". Their relationship ended in 1964. In 2008, Rotolo published a memoir about her life in Greenwich Village and her relationship with Dylan in the 1960s, A Freewheelin' Time.

Joan Baez first met Dylan in April 1961, after she'd released her first album, being acclaimed as the "Queen of Folk". On hearing Dylan perform his song "With God on Our Side," Baez later said, "I never thought anything so powerful could come out of that little toad". In July 1963, Baez invited Dylan to join her on stage at the Newport Folk Festival, setting the scene for similar duets over the next two years.

By the time of Dylan's 1965 tour of the U.K, their romantic relationship had begun to fizzle out, as captured in D. A. Pennebaker's documentary film Dont Look Back. Baez later toured with Dylan as a performer on his Rolling Thunder Revue in 1975–76, singing four songs with Dylan on the live album of the tour, Bob Dylan Live 1975, The Rolling Thunder Revue.

Baez appeared with Dylan in the one-hour TV special Hard Rain, filmed at Fort Collins, Colorado, in May 1976. She also starred as 'The Woman In White,' in the film Renaldo and Clara

(1978), directed by Dylan and filmed during the Rolling Thunder Revue. Dylan and Baez toured together again in 1984, with Carlos Santana.

Baez recalled her relationship with Dylan in Martin Scorsese's documentary film, No Direction Home (2005). She wrote about Dylan in two autobiographies, admiringly in Daybreak (1968), then less admiringly in And A Voice to Sing With (1987). Baez's relationship with Dylan was the subject of her song "Diamonds & Rust", which has been described as "an acute portrait" of Dylan.

Dylan married Sara Lownds, who had worked as a model and a secretary to Drew Associates, on November 22, 1965. Their first child, Jesse Byron Dylan, was born on January 6, 1966, with the couple going on to have three more children: Anna Lea (born July 11, 1967), Samuel Isaac Abram (born July 30, 1968), and Jakob Luke (born December 9, 1969). Dylan also adopted Sara's daughter from a prior marriage, Maria Lownds (later Dylan, born October 21, 1961). Sara Dylan played the role of Clara, in Dylan's film Renaldo and Clara (1978). Bob and Sara Dylan were divorced on June 29, 1977.

Maria married musician Peter Himmelman in 1988. In the 1990s, Jakob became well known as the lead singer of the band the Wallflowers; Jesse is a film director and a successful businessman.

Dylan married his backup singer Carolyn Dennis, professionally known by her maiden name, on June 4, 1986. Desiree Gabrielle Dennis-Dylan, their daughter had been born on January 31, 1986. The couple divorced in October 1992, their marriage and child having remained a closely guarded secret, until the publication of Howard Sounes' biography, Down the Highway: The Life of Bob Dylan, in 2001.

When not touring, Dylan mainly lives in Point Dume, a promontory on the coast of Malibu, California, though he owns other property around the world.

Growing up in Hibbing, Minnesota, Dylan and his family were part of the area's small but close-knit Jewish community, in May 1954 Dylan having his Bar Mitzvah. Around the time of his 30th birthday, in 1971, Dylan visited Israel, meeting Rabbi Meir Kahane, founder of the New York-based Jewish Defense League. Time magazine quoted him saying about Kahane, "He's a really sincere guy. He's really put it all together," but subsequently, Dylan downplayed the extent of his contact with Kahane.

During the late 1970s, Dylan converted to Christianity. In November 1978, guided by his friend Mary Alice Artes, Dylan made contact with the Vineyard School of Discipleship. Vineyard Pastor Kenn Gulliksen recalled: "Larry Myers and Paul Emond went over to Bob's house and ministered to him. He responded by saying, 'Yes he did in fact want Christ in his life,' and he prayed that day and received the Lord." From January to March 1979, Dylan attended the Vineyard Bible study classes in Reseda, California.

By 1984, Dylan was distancing himself from the "born again" label. He told Kurt Loder of Rolling Stone magazine: "I've never said I'm born again. That's just a media term. I don't think I've been an agnostic. I've always thought there's a superior power, that this is not the real world and that there's a world to come." In response to Loder's asking whether he belonged to any church or synagogue, Dylan laughingly replied, "Not really. Uh, the Church of the Poison Mind." In 1997, he told David Gates of Newsweek:

"Here's the thing with me and the religious thing. This is the flat-out truth: I find the religiosity and philosophy in the music. I don't find it anywhere else. Songs like "Let Me Rest on a Peaceful Mountain" or "I Saw the Light"—that's my religion. I don't adhere to rabbis, preachers, evangelists, all of that. I've learned more from the songs than I've learned from any of this kind of entity. The songs are my lexicon. I believe the songs."

In an interview published in The New York Times on September 28, 1997, journalist Jon Pareles reported that "Dylan says he now subscribes to no organized religion."

Dylan has supported the Chabad Lubavitch movement, and has privately participated in Jewish religious events, including the Bar Mitzvahs of his sons and attending Hadar Hatorah, a Chabad Lubavitch yeshiva. In September 1989 and September 1991, he appeared on the Chabad telethon. On Yom Kippur in 2007, he attended Congregation Beth Tefillah, in Atlanta, Georgia, where he was called to the Torah for the sixth aliyah.

Dylan has continued to perform songs from his gospel albums in concert, occasionally covering traditional religious songs. He has also made passing references to his religious faith—such as in a 2004 interview with 60 Minutes, when he told Ed Bradley that "the only person you have to think twice about lying to,is either yourself or to God." He also explained his constant touring schedule, as part of a bargain he made a long time ago with the "chief commander—in this earth and in the world we can't see."

In a 2009 interview with Bill Flanagan, promoting Dylan's Christmas LP, Christmas in the Heart, Flanagan commented on the "heroic performance" Dylan gave of "O Little Town of Bethlehem," saying that he "delivered the song like a true believer". Dylan replied: "Well, I am a true believer."

Dylan has won many awards throughout his career, including the 2016 Nobel Prize in Literature, twelve Grammy Awards, one Academy Award and one Golden Globe Award. He has been inducted into the Rock and Roll Hall of Fame, Nashville Songwriters Hall of Fame, and

Songwriters Hall of Fame. In May 2000, Dylan received the Polar Music Prize from Sweden's King Carl XVI.

In June 2007, Dylan received the Prince of Asturias Award in the Arts category. Dylan received the Presidential Medal of Freedom in May 2012. In February 2015, Dylan accepted the MusiCares Person of the Year award, from the National Academy of Recording Arts and Sciences, in recognition of his philanthropic and artistic contributions to society. In November 2013, Dylan received the accolade of Légion d'Honneur, from the French education minister Aurélie Filippetti.

The Nobel Prize committee announced on October 13, 2016, that it would be awarding Dylan the Nobel Prize in Literature "for having created new poetic expressions within the great American song tradition". The New York Times reported: "Mr. Dylan, 75, is the first musician to win the award, and his selection on Thursday, is perhaps the most radical choice in a history stretching back to 1901."

On October 21, a member of the Swedish Academy, writer Per Wästberg, termed Dylan "rude and arrogant," for ignoring the Nobel Committee's attempts to contact him. Academy permanent secretary Sara Danius stated, "The Swedish Academy has never held a view on a prizewinner's decision in this context, neither will it now."

After two weeks of speculation about Dylan's silence concerning the Nobel Prize, he said in an interview with Edna Gundersen that getting the award was: "amazing, incredible. Whoever dreams about something like that?"

On November 17, the Swedish Academy announced that Dylan would not travel to Stockholm for the Nobel Prize Ceremony, due to "pre-existing commitments". At the Nobel Banquet in Stockholm on December 10, 2016, Dylan's banquet speech was given by Azita Raji, U.S. Ambassador to Sweden.

The speech stated: "From an early age, I've been familiar with and reading and absorbing the works of those who were deemed worthy of such a distinction: Kipling, Shaw, Thomas Mann, Pearl Buck, Albert Camus, Hemingway. These giants of literature, whose works are taught in the schoolroom, housed in libraries around the world and spoken of in reverent tones, have always made a deep impression. That I now join the names on such a list is truly beyond words." Patti Smith accepted Dylan's Nobel prize with a "transcendent performance" of his song "A Hard Rain's A-Gonna Fall" to orchestral accompaniment.

On April 2, 2017, the Academy secretary Danius said: "Earlier today the Swedish Academy met with Bob Dylan for a private ceremony [with no media present] in Stockholm, during which Dylan received his gold medal and diploma. Twelve members of the Academy were present. Spirits were high. Champagne was had.

Quite a bit of time was spent looking closely at the gold medal, in particular the beautifully crafted back, an image of a young man sitting under a laurel tree, who listens to the Muse. Taken from Virgil's Aeneid, the inscription reads: Inventas vitam iuvat excoluisse per artes, loosely translated as "And they who bettered life on earth by their newly found mastery."

On June 5, 2017, Dylan's Nobel Lecture was posted on the Nobel prize website. The New York Times pointed out that, in order to collect the prize's 8 million Swedish krona ($900,000), the Swedish Academy's rules stipulate that the laureate "must deliver a lecture within six months of the official ceremony, which would have made Mr. Dylan's deadline June 10."

Academy secretary Danius commented: "The speech is extraordinary and, as one might expect, eloquent. Now that the lecture has been delivered, the Dylan adventure is coming to a close." In his essay, Dylan wrote about the impact that three important books had made on him: Herman Melville's Moby Dick, Erich Maria Remarque's All Quiet on the Western Front and Homer's The Odyssey.

He concluded: "Our songs are alive in the land of the living but songs are unlike literature, they're meant to be sung, not read. The words in Shakespeare's plays were meant to be acted on the stage, just as lyrics in songs are meant to be sung, not read on a page and I hope some of you get the chance to listen to these lyrics, the way they were intended to be heard: in concert or on record or however people are listening to songs these days. I return once again to Homer, who says, 'Sing in me, oh Muse, and through me tell the story'." Alan Pasqua provided the uncredited piano accompaniment for the recorded speech.

Dylan has been described as one of the most influential figures of the 20th century, musically and culturally. He was included in the Time 100: The Most Important People of the Century, where he was called "master poet, caustic social critic and intrepid, guiding spirit of the counterculture generation".

In 2008, The Pulitzer Prize jury awarded him a special citation for "his profound impact on popular music and American culture, marked by lyrical compositions of extraordinary poetic power." President Barack Obama said of Dylan in 2012, "There is not a bigger giant in the history of American music."

For 20 years, academics lobbied the Swedish Academy to give Dylan the Nobel Prize in Literature, which awarded it to him in 2016, making Dylan the first musician to be awarded the Literature Prize. Horace Engdahl, a member of the Nobel Committee, described Dylan's place in literary history:

"...a singer worthy of a place beside the Greek bards, beside Ovid, beside the Romantic visionaries, beside the kings and queens of the blues, beside the forgotten masters of brilliant standards."

Rolling Stone ranked Dylan at # 1 in its 2015 list of the 100 Greatest Songwriters of All Time, having listed "Like A Rolling Stone," as the "Greatest Song of all Time" in 2011. In 2008, it was estimated that Dylan had sold about 120 million albums worldwide.

I loved him, because he wrote some beautiful stuff. I used to love his so-called protest things but I like the sound of him. I didn't have to listen to his words. He used to come with his acetate and say, "Listen to this, John. Did you hear the words?" And I said, "That doesn't matter, just the sound is what counts. The overall thing." You didn't have to hear what Bob Dylan's saying, you just have to hear the way he says it, like the medium is the message...I respected him, I respected him a lot".

John Lennon, 1970

Initially modeling his writing style on the songs of Woody Guthrie, the blues of Robert Johnson, and what he termed the "architectural forms" of Hank Williams songs, Dylan added increasingly sophisticated lyrical techniques to the folk music of the early 1960s, infusing it "with the intellectualism of classic literature and poetry".

Paul Simon suggested that Dylan's early compositions virtually took over the folk genre: "[Dylan's] early songs were very rich ... with strong melodies. 'Blowin' in the Wind' has a really strong melody. He so enlarged himself through the folk background that he incorporated it for a while. He defined the genre for a while."

When Dylan made his move from acoustic folk and blues music to a rock backing, the mix became more complex. For many critics, his greatest achievement was the cultural synthesis exemplified by his mid-1960s trilogy of albums—Bringing It All Back Home, Highway 61 Revisited and Blonde on Blonde. In Mike Marqusee's words:

"Between late 1964 and the middle of 1966, Dylan created a body of work that remains unique. Drawing on folk, blues, country, R&B, rock'n'roll, gospel, British beat, symbolist, modernist and Beat poetry, surrealism and Dada, advertising jargon and social commentary, Fellini and Mad magazine, he forged a coherent and original artistic voice and vision. The beauty of these albums retains the power to shock and console."

Dylan's lyrics began to receive detailed scrutiny from academics and poets in 1998, when

Stanford University sponsored the first international academic conference on Bob Dylan to be held in the United States. In 2004, Richard F. Thomas, Classics professor at Harvard University, created a freshman seminar titled "Dylan," "to put the artist in context of not just popular culture of the last half-century, but the tradition of classical poets like Virgil and Homer."

William Arctander O'Brien, literary scholar and professor of German and Comparative Literature, at the University of California, San Diego, memorialized the significance of Dylan's contribution to world literature, when he created a full academic course in 2009 devoted to Dylan, which analyzed and celebrated the "historical, political, economic, aesthetic, and cultural significance of Dylan's work."

Literary critic Christopher Ricks, published 'Dylan's Visions of Sin', a 500-page analysis of Dylan's work, having said: "I'd not have written a book about Dylan, to stand alongside my books on Milton and Keats, Tennyson and T.S. Eliot, if I didn't think Dylan a genius of and with language. Former British poet laureate Andrew Motion, suggested his lyrics should be studied in schools. The critical consensus that Dylan's song writing was his outstanding creative achievement, was articulated by Encyclopædia Britannica, where his entry stated: "Hailed as the Shakespeare of his generation, Dylan... set the standard for lyric writing."

Dylan's voice also received critical attention. New York Times critic Robert Shelton described his early vocal style as "a rusty voice, suggesting Guthrie's old performances, etched in gravel like Dave Van Ronk's." David Bowie, in his tribute, "Song for Bob Dylan", described Dylan's singing as "a voice like sand and glue".

His voice continued to develop as he began to work with rock'n'roll backing bands; critic Michael Gray described the sound of Dylan's vocal work on "Like a Rolling Stone," as "at once young and jeeringly cynical". As Dylan's voice aged during the 1980s, for some critics, it became more expressive.

Christophe Lebold wrote in the journal Oral Tradition, "Dylan's more recent broken voice, enables him to present a world view at the sonic surface of the songs—this voice carries us across the landscape of a broken, fallen world. The anatomy of a broken world in "Everything is Broken" (on the album Oh Mercy) is but an example of how the thematic concern with all things broken, is grounded in a concrete sonic reality."

Dylan is considered a seminal influence on many musical genres. As Edna Gundersen stated in USA Today: "Dylan's musical DNA, has informed nearly every simple twist of pop since 1962." Punk musician Joe Strummer praised Dylan, for having "laid down the template for lyric, tune, seriousness, spirituality, depth of rock music."

Other major musicians who have acknowledged Dylan's importance include Johnny Cash, Jerry Garcia, John Lennon, Paul McCartney, Pete Townshend, Neil Young, Bruce Springsteen,

David Bowie, Bryan Ferry, Nick Cave, Patti Smith, Syd Barrett, Joni Mitchell, Tom Waits and Leonard Cohen.

Dylan significantly contributed to the initial success of both the Byrds and the Band: the Byrds achieved chart success with their version of "Mr. Tambourine Man" and the subsequent album, while the Band were Dylan's backing band on his 1966 tour, recording The Basement Tapes with him in 1967, featuring three previously unreleased Dylan songs on their debut album.

Some critics have dissented from the view of Dylan as a visionary figure in popular music. In his book Awopbopaloobop Alopbamboom, Nik Cohn objected: "I can't take the vision of Dylan as seer, as teenage messiah, as everything else he's been worshipped as. The way I see him, he's a minor talent with a major gift for self-hype."

Australian critic Jack Marx credited Dylan with changing the persona of the rock star: "What cannot be disputed is that Dylan invented the arrogant, faux-cerebral posturing that has been the dominant style in rock since, with everyone from Mick Jagger to Eminem educating themselves from the Dylan handbook."

Fellow musicians have also presented dissenting views. Joni Mitchell described Dylan as a "plagiarist" and his voice as "fake," in a 2010 interview in the Los Angeles Times, despite Mitchell having toured with Dylan in the past, and both artists having covered each others songs.

Mitchell's comments led to discussions of Dylan's use of other people's material, both supporting and criticizing him. Talking to Mikal Gilmore in Rolling Stone in 2012, Dylan responded to the allegation of plagiarism, including his use of Henry Timrod's verse in his album Modern Times, by saying that it was "part of the tradition".

If Dylan's work during the 1960s, was seen as bringing intellectual ambition to popular music, critics in the 21st century have described him as a figure, who had greatly expanded the folk culture from which he initially emerged. Following the release of Todd Haynes' Dylan biopic I'm Not There, J. Hoberman wrote in his 2007 Village Voice review:

"Elvis might never have been born, but someone else would surely have brought the world rock 'n' roll. No such logic accounts for Bob Dylan. No iron law of history demanded that a would-be Elvis from Hibbing, Minnesota, would swerve through the Greenwich Village folk revival, to become the world's first and greatest rock 'n' roll beatnik bard and then—having achieved fame and adoration beyond reckoning—vanish into a folk tradition of his own making."

When Dylan was awarded the Nobel Prize in Literature, The New York Times commented: "In choosing a popular musician for the literary world's highest honour, the Swedish Academy, which awards the prize, dramatically redefined the boundaries of literature, setting off a debate about whether song lyrics have the same artistic value as poetry or novels."

Responses varied from the sarcasm of Irvine Welsh, who described it as "an ill conceived nostalgia award, wrenched from the rancid prostates of senile, gibbering hippies", to the enthusiasm of Salman Rushdie who tweeted: "From Orpheus to Faiz, song & poetry have been closely linked. Dylan is the brilliant inheritor of the bardic tradition. Great choice."

Dylan's archive, comprising notebooks, song drafts, business contracts, recordings and movie out-takes, are held at the Gilcrease Museum's Helmerich Center for American Research, in Tulsa, Oklahoma, which is also the home of the archives for Woody Guthrie. While selections from the archive may be consulted at the Helmerich Center, the George Kaiser Family Foundation has announced a design competition for a major Bob Dylan Center in Tulsa's Arts District.

In 2005, 7th Avenue East in Hibbing, Minnesota, the street on which Dylan lived from the age of 6 to 18, received the honorary name Bob Dylan Drive. In the town Hibbing, a walk of fame-styled "star" is embedded in a sidewalk, with the words Bob Dylan, as well as a cursive-Z for Dylan's nickname Zimmy in his youth.

In 2006 a cultural pathway, Bob Dylan Way, was inaugurated in Duluth, Minnesota, the city where Dylan was born. The 1.8 mile path links "cultural and historically significant areas of downtown for the tourists". In 2015, a massive Bob Dylan mural was unveiled in downtown Minneapolis, the city where Dylan attended university for a year. The mural was designed by Brazilian street artist Eduardo Kobra.

Made in the USA
Lexington, KY
03 June 2018